INSIGHT HERITAGE GUIDES

THE MALTA MARITIME MUSEUM

Vittoriosa

EMMANUEL MAGRO CONTI

PHOTOGRAPHY
DANIEL CILIA

HERITAGE BOOKS
IN ASSOCIATION WITH
Heritage Malta
2006

HOW TO GET TO THE MARITIME MUSEUM

By bus:
Bus nos. 1, 2, 4, 6 from Valletta main bus terminus and stop at Vittoriosa bus terminus.

By car:
Main roads leading to the Three Cities and then follow the road signs to Vittoriosa and the Maritime Museum.

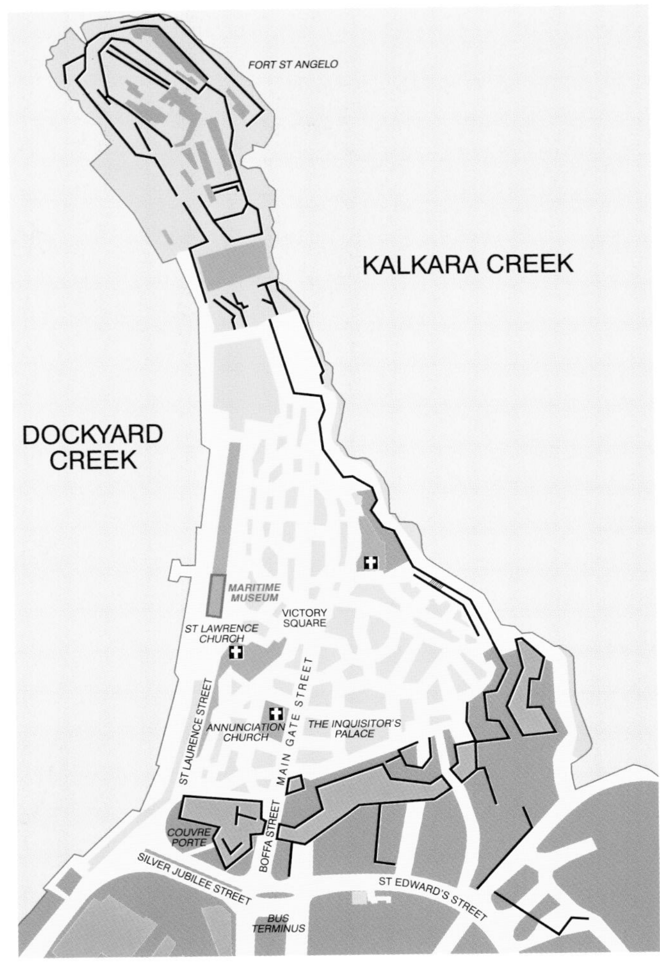

Malta Maritime Museum
Ex-Naval Bakery
Vittoriosa CSP 08

Tel: 2180 5287
www.heritagemalta.org

This series is supported by:

Insight Heritage Guides Series No: 11
General Editor: Louis J. Scerri

Published by Heritage Books, a subsidiary of Midsea Books Ltd, Carmelites Street, Sta Venera HMR 11, Malta
sales@midseabooks.com

Insight Heritage Guides is a series of books intended to give an insight into aspects and sites of Malta's rich heritage, culture, and traditions.

Produced by Mizzi Design & Graphic Services
Printed by Gutenberg Press

First published 2006
ISBN: 99932-7-075-X

BACKGROUND OF THE MALTA MARITIME MUSEUM

The Malta Maritime Museum was officially opened to the public on 24 July 1992 by the then minister responsible for Education and Museums, Dr Ugo Mifsud Bonnici, four years after the inception of the idea. An advisory committee had been set up in 1988 to assist in the setting up of the Maritime Museum and during these years several artefacts were collected from various sources.[1] A suitable building, large enough to cater for the large maritime exhibits, was identified in the former Royal Naval Bakery at Vittoriosa, which met all the set requirements and which was then a derelict building.

Detail of the facade of the Naval Bakery which now houses the Malta Maritime Museum

THE ARSENAL

The Order of St John built and maintained its galley fleet inside the Arsenal. A large galley shed was built on the present Malta Maritime Museum site in 1607 during the grandmastership of Alof de Wignacourt (1601-22) replacing an older galley shed possibly close to Fort St Angelo.[2] A few years later a second shed was built adjoining the first one on the site of two houses donated by Fra Agostino Mego.[3] In 1636, a third galley shed was built abutting the other two sheds with funds donated by the Prior of Toulouse Fra Dallins and the Knight Fra Antonio Scalamonte[4] during the grandmastership of Jean Paul de Lascaris Casteller (1636-57). In 1667 during the grandmastership of Nicholas Cottoner (1663-80) the wooden roofs of the arsenal were replaced.[5] During the grandmastership of Fra Adrian de Wignacourt (1690-97) the arsenal was partly restored and partly built anew.[6]

Period paintings, drawings, and engravings of the Arsenal after the 1690s interventions illustrate an ordered façade with coat-of-arms, balustrades, and statuary. These sources gain further importance since they are the only visual documents of the demolished building.

The galley arsenal arches and slipways beneath them were built slanted in the direction of the mouth of the *Porto delle Galere* (Dockyard Creek). This is testified by a singular plan of the site drawn by William Scamp of the site with his proposed Naval Bakery footprint superimposed on the existing Arsenal footprint.[7] This slanting assisted the galley-builders mainly in the slipping out of galleys from the Arsenal towards more open waters inside the creek. Had the arches and the slips been built at right angles with the rest of the *Marina Grande* buildings, the launched galleys ran the risk of being immediately shipwrecked against Senglea.

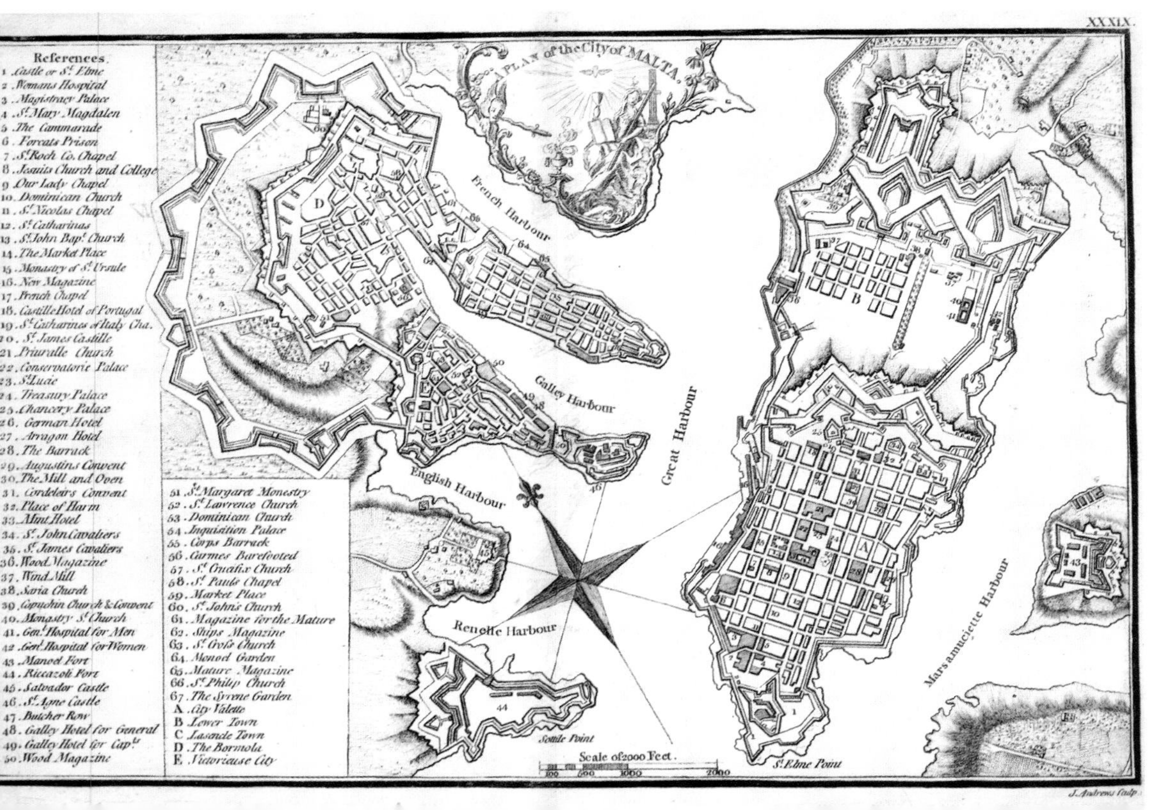

Map of the Grand Harbour by J. Andrews, late 18th century

THE NAVAL BAKERY

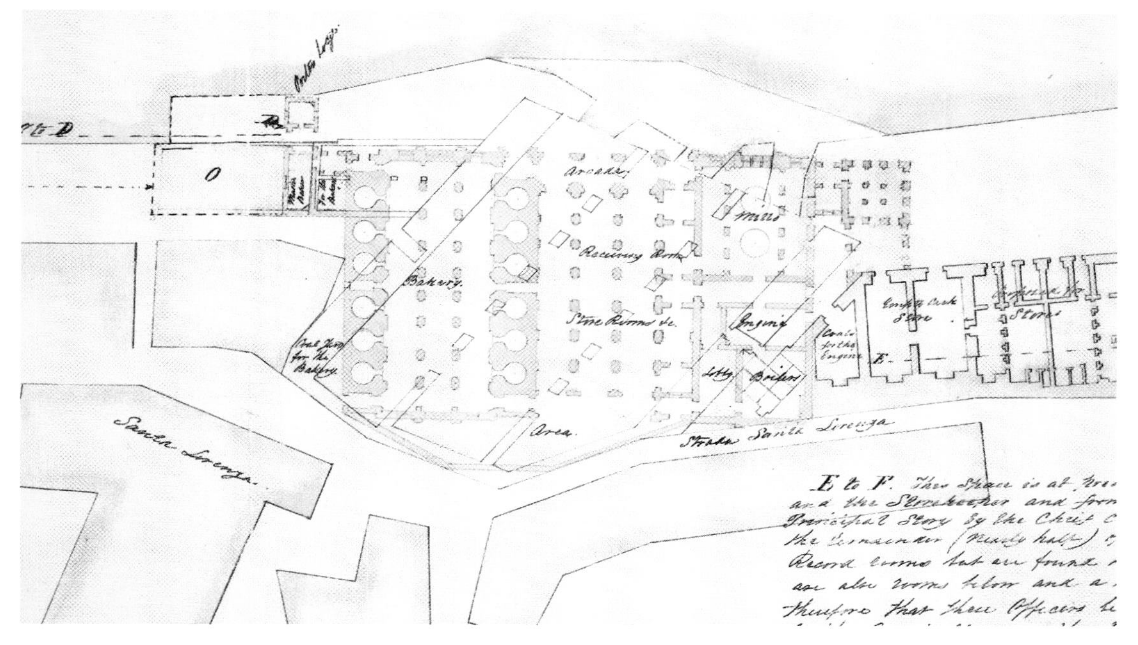

Plan of the proposed new bakery, by William Scamp, superimposed over the then existing Order's Arsenal

The naval bakery supplied the Royal Navy's Mediterranean fleet stationed in Malta with its daily requirements of bread and biscuits. The bakery was designed by the British architect and engineer William Scamp and was built between 1842 and 1845 on the site of the Galley Arsenal of the Order of St John which was demolished in 1842.[7] The choice of place was dictated by the need to have the bakery in the very hub of the Victualling Yard. In his overall design for the façade, Scamp was inspired by the façade of Windsor Castle in England. The arrangement of the façade doors in the first and second floors, grouped together by means of a single recessed giant arch with the openings guarded by means of a balustrade is, to say the least, a direct copy of Windsor Castle's façade. A then novel innovation in Maltese architecture was the introduction of cast-iron columns in parts of the building as supports for subsequent roofing structures and of rolled steel joists instead of timber beams for roofing various floors.

The bakery's steam-driven machinery was operated for the first time on 10 April 1845.[8] Coal necessary for the firing of the boiler's furnaces which operated the bakery's machinery was stored in the adjoining sixteenth-century Treasury building, which building was integrated in the overall design as part and parcel of the bakery as stores including grain and coal. When inaugurated in 1848, the naval bakery represented the very height of Victorian technology. Two 25 horse-power steam-driven engines were used to wash, dry, and grind the grain into flour by means of eight sets of trashing mills. These engines were also used to power machinery to mix, roll, and stamp out the biscuits. Working round the clock, the total production of the naval bakery

MISSION OF THE MUSEUM

The Museum aims at illustrating Malta's maritime history from prehistory to the present day and to illustrate the fascination of the sea within the Mediterranean context, without neglecting the overall global nature of seafaring. These aims are achieved by the constant search for, identification, and acquisition of artefacts related to the museum's mission. This task has been aided by the constant donations over these past years by the Maltese general public, foreign individuals, companies, corporate bodies, foreign maritime and naval museums, foreign navies, and Maltese and foreign ambassadors and high amounted to 30,000 lbs. of bread and biscuits a day.[9]

In another part of the building were twelve ovens installed between 1847 and 1848, also coal-fired. Six of these ovens were totally dismantled possibly after the Second World War, whilst the other six survive practically intact, except for the interior of one of them. Above these ovens are passages in which biscuits, known in naval jargon as 'hard tack', were dried by means of the oven heat comimg from below. Amongst British victualling yard bakeries, these ovens are unique, since those at Devonport and Portsmouth have long since been removed. The latter bakeries themselves had been closed down by 1907.[10] The Malta bakery ceased to function in the 1950s and was converted into offices and stores and subsequently into the headquarters of the Admiralty Constabulary. The 'Bakery', as it was and still is affectionately known, remained part of the Royal Naval establishments up to the closure of the British base on 31 March 1979.

Two of several grinding stones dating to the mid-1840s found burried in a pit in the Mill Room, now the Anadian Hall

Various parts of the Bakery were damaged during the Second World War. All of the façades, turrets, and the clock tower are still scarred by splinter marks. In the 1950s, the Baker's House and Offices were pulled down to create an open space in front of St Lawrence Collegiate Parish Church. The on-going restoration programme includes the reconstruction of various parts destroyed during the Second World War.

One of the 12 ovens built during the 1840s in the Bakery Hall

THE CLOCK TOWER

A prominent feature in the bakery building is the clock tower, a typical feature in victualling yards and dockyards. Amongst the Maltese naval establishments, this particular turret clock is the oldest of all. It bears the maker's plate of Matthew Dutton of London[11] with the date 1810, which actually predates the bakery building itself.[12]

The clock movement is also stamped 'Suban Malta' on various parts.[13] The clockwork was originally designed to have four clock faces; however, the clock tower as designed

The clock tower with the War Department bell cast in 1790

by Scamp was meant to have only three faces, the fourth side being utilized as a large window to permit natural light inside the clock movement platform. Three bells strike the hours and the quarters, the two-quarter bells dated 1810, and the hour's bell dated 1790 are marked with the arrow mark of the War Department. All bells are by the Mears Foundry of London, and are the oldest British bells in Malta.[14]

The clock engine and details (above and below) of the mechanism, included toothed wheels (left) with the inscription 'Bros. Suban Malta 1896' indicating restoration works carried out on the clock's mechanism

TOUR OF THE MUSEUM

Presently, the museum covers over 2,000 sq.m., some 30 per cent of the total floor area available. An ongoing building rehabilitation and restoration programme is linked with the opening of new halls or sections devoted to specific maritime themes or chronological periods. After the museum's inauguration in 1992 by means of a hall of 600 sq.m., another 800 sq.m. hall was inaugurated in November 2000 dedicated entirely to the Royal Navy in Malta. The former hall was then dedicated to the Order of St John period. In October 2003, another section was opened spread over two levels of 250 sq.m. each dedicated to marine engineering. Five smaller halls and sections are devoted to ancient shipping, navigation, the merchant navy, Maltese traditional boats, and Maltese customs and water police. These are just token displays of the museum's collections on the subjects, which will eventually move to larger halls when rehabilitation and restoration works are completed. Other halls would be dedicated to port facilities, maritime-related sports, and the Armed Forces of the Malta Maritime Squadron.[15]

ANCIENT SHIPPING

General view of the ancient shipping section, showing Roman lead stock anchors and amphoras. Panels describe ancient navigation by means of illustrations and models

The ancient shipping section includes a small collection of ancient ship models, both merchant vessels, such as a Roman grain ship, and war vessels, such as a Greek trireme.[16] Also exhibited are various watercolours of other various ancient ships. A few amphorae are on display together with a collection of authentic Roman lead stock anchors. The latter collection includes a reconstruction of a Roman anchor, which reconstruction incorporates a Roman lead stock anchor. All these items were retrieved from Maltese territorial waters. A small display treating the shipwreck of St Paul in AD 60 at Malta concludes the Ancient Shipping display.

In future the museum will incorporate a 450 sq.m. hall entirely dedicated to seafaring in the Mediterranean with an emphasis on maritime affairs in and around Maltese waters during the prehistoric, classical, and medieval periods. The focus will be on migration and trade to and from the Maltese islands during these periods.

Opposite: The third-rate Order's Nautical School instruction model for rigging and hull construction

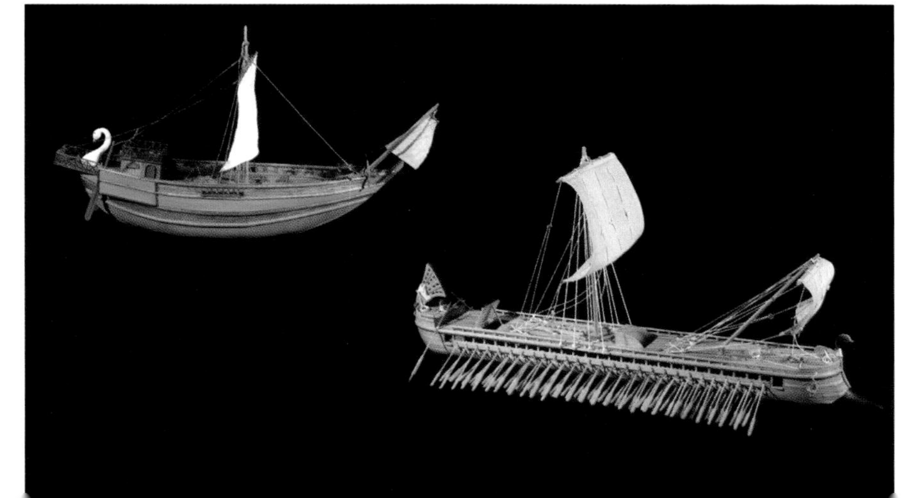

Two classical period models: a Roman grain ship and a Greek trireme

THE ORDER OF ST JOHN

The naval vicissitudes of the Order of St John between 1530 and 1798 are strongly tied with Malta. This glorious period is represented by a host of various historical items. A small but important collection of authentic period models, some originally pertaining to the *Congregazione delle Galere* and to the Order's nautical school, is on display. It features the main types of the Order's naval ceremonial ships and boats.

Grand Master Ramon Perellos y Roccaful (1697-1720)

An Order of St John naval battle scene, showing the square-sail squadron in action against the 'Padrona di Tunis' on 3 May 1706

S LI 3 MAG. 1706
A DALA SCUA
M E FRC CA S PI
E FVGE

The unplanked starboard side of the third-rate Order's Nautical School model

The galley model

The *mezza-galera* model

A late eighteenth-century *mezza-galera* together with a full galley model illustrate the main fighting warships of the Order up to the beginning of the eighteenth century. Two large eighteenth-century third rate models once pertaining to the Order's Nautical School document the ships-of-the-line squadron, introduced in 1702 by Grand Master Ramon Perellos y Roccaful (1697-1720) to complement the galley squadron. The larger of these two models was mainly intended to demonstrate the standing and running rigging. Each deck of the smaller model explodes into sections to demonstrate the construction and various divisions of a typical third rate ship-of-the-line.

A *Xambek* model concludes the fighting ship models section. *Xam-*

beks were mostly used by licensed Maltese corsairs flying the colours of the Order of St John. The vessel type itself was North African in origin but was skilfully adapted by many western Mediterranean countries for corsairing operations. Maltese corsairs sold shares to individuals prior to a *corso*. This lucrative trade inspired many Maltese residents into such a business either as *padroni* of the vessels themselves or else by buying shares in such operations. Particular knights of the Order of St John were also lured into these activities by buying shares and also taking part in the *corso*. Shareholders included none other than the cloistered nuns of St Ursola at Valletta, the female branch of the Order of St John.

Two authentic ceremonial boat models show the affluence of decoration on the grand master's stately boats. The oldest is the 'gondola' of Grand Master Adrian de Wignacourt (1690-97)[17] and the other is the brigantine barge of Grand Master Antonio Manoel de Vilhena (1722-36). Another early eighteenth-century ceremonial boat model is the *felucca dorata*[18] pertaining to the Captain General of the Galleys, which still retains its original paintwork and drapery curtains.

Several period oil paintings, watercolours, and engravings dating between the sixteenth and the eighteenth century, pictorially illustrate the Order's sea battles, campaigns, and other important events. A large *ex-voto* panel painting by Antonello Ricci commemorates the Battle of Lepanto (1571), the last major encounter between galleys in the Mediterranean. This is the oldest painting in the museum's collection and illustrates the Catholic and Ottoman fleets in battle order, including the Order's galley squadron, with a knight of the Order of St

Top: A naval battle scene in which the galley and the square-sail squadrons of the Order's Navy participated in tandem to overwhelm the enemy
Above left: The *Xambekk* model
Above right: A model of the ceremonial barge belonging to Grand Master Antonio Manoel de Vilhena (1722-36)

A model of the ceremonial gondola belonging to Grand Master Alof de Wignacourt (1690-97)

Left: The Lepanto ex-voto panel

A late 18th-century painting showing the Valletta marina

John kneeling in prayer invoking Our Lady, the Child Jesus, St Lucy, and St John. Charming little details include angels and devils hovering around the galleys of the Christian League and the Ottomans respectively. The only Christian galley identified by name, the *San Pietro*, was the one on which the grateful donor of the *ex voto* presumably served.

Sea battle scenes illustrate the fighting tactics of the Order's two squadrons in narrative type paintings. One of the most delightful paintings is a view of the Valletta marina, pregnant with details of the various maritime aspects of Maltese trade and commerce as seen by a mid-eighteenth-century anonymous painter. Two monochrome watercolours depict the funerals held in Malta in 1792 of the Venetian Admiral Angelo Emo who died in Malta. A series of engravings represent the Peloponnese campaign of 1686 under the command of the then Order's Captain General of the Galleys Fra Johann Josef Von Herbernstein. Portraits of some of the Order's most distinguished naval personalities on exhibit, include that of Fra Paul-Julien de Suffren de Saint Tropez, captain of one of the Order's galleys.

A thematic section in the Order of St John hall deals with shipbuilding and repairs of the Order's navy. Prominently featured in this section are the marble Salvago and the Amati arsenal

Fra Paul-Julien de Suffren de Saint Tropez (1730-1806)

memorials. The stern model of the third rate *San Gioacchino* dated 1768 with the coat-of-arms of Grand Master Manoel Pinto de Fonseca (1741-73) is the only dockyard model pertaining to the Order's navy known to have survived. The two dioramas demonstrate the caulking of a galley and the sheer or *macina* bastion in use to illustrate the practice of caulking and the use of the

Opposite below: Detail from a monochrome watercolour showing the funeral cortege at the Grand Harbour of Admiral Angelo Emo, 1792

Left: A diorama model showing the rigging of masts at the Order's shipyards
Below: A diorama model showing the caulking of galleys

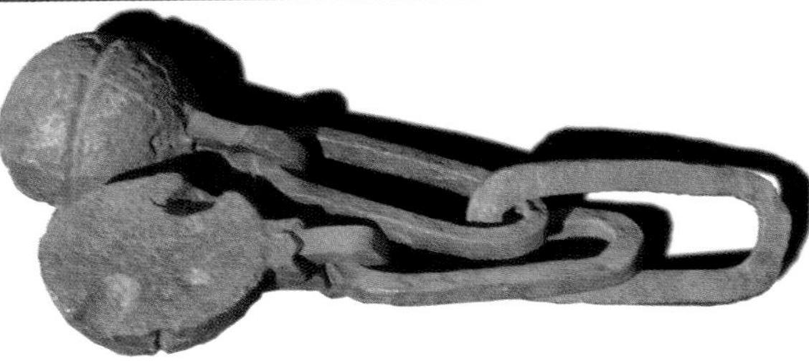

sheer bastion to remove or replace ships-of-the-line masts.

A small selection of edged weapons, firearms, and cannon, used on the Order's warships are exhibited. A selection of Spanish pikes, boarding pikes, rapiers, and hangers document the various

Top: General view of the arms section in the Order of St John's Naval Hall

Above: A chain-shot, 18th century

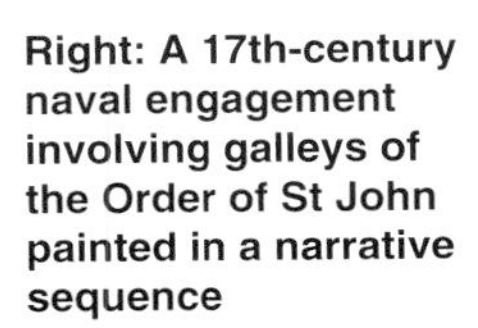

Right: A 17th-century naval engagement involving galleys of the Order of St John painted in a narrative sequence

A small gun and shots from the Order's navy

fighting tactics adopted by the Order's naval fighting forces. The North African Muslim *saif* and *kilji* swords on display are actually sea-battle trophies. A sawn-off musket, inscribed *Galere de France*, together with a pistol, complete the personal arms section. Various ceremonial petard launchers document the joyous festivities celebrated in Maltese harbours by the Order's warships on their return after each successful campaign. A selection of Order-period bronze and iron naval guns together with various types of cannon shot and an extremely rare chain shot, which was used to disable the enemy by hacking up masts and rigging, are exhibited. The museum possesses the only two breech-loading guns existing in Malta, both of which are made of iron. One is stave built and dates to the sixteenth century and the other dates to two centuries later. Another thematic section in the Order of St John Hall deals with naval artillery treatises and instruments used by the gunners of the Order. One of the gunners' rulers on display is decorated with the effigy of St Barbara, patron saint of the bombardiers, the gunners of the Order's ships.

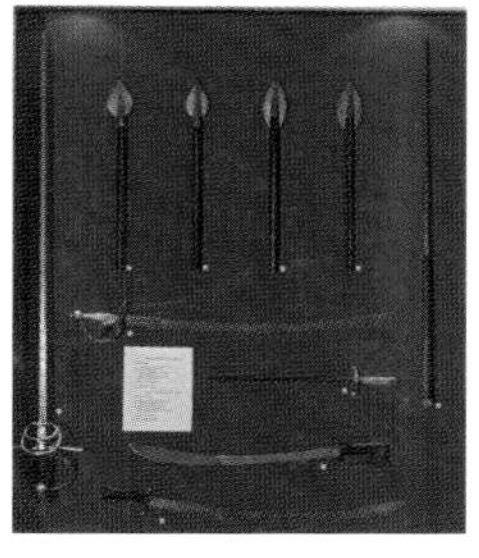

Edged weapons used on the Order's Naval Units including the long four-sided boarding pike and the two swords, trophies from naval engagements

Another model from the Order's nautical school which opens in several sections to reveal compartments and different levels of the ship

FRENCH PERIOD

The section of the French interlude (1798-1800) is located between the Order of St John hall and the Royal Navy hall. Two large French republican guns, a prisoner-of-war wooden model of the French second rater *Bucentaur*, documents, edged period weapons, and a host of water colours, engravings, and lithographs including portraits, illustrate these two eventful years. Amongst the portraits are two period plaques, one a Sevres bisque of Napoleon and the other a Wedgwood jasper of Nelson.

A French prisoner-of-war model of the Bucentaur, the French flagship in 1805 duri the Battle of Trafalgar of 4 October 1805

Sevres plaque with Napoleon's profile

'Prise de Malte', engraving showing Napoleon Bonaparte being rowed to Malta from *L'Orient*

BRITISH PERIOD

The British period in Malta (1798-1979)[19] is documented with various paintings, watercolours, engravings, period models, uniforms, and a host of various artefacts. The hall is divided into various sections illustrating the role of the Royal Navy in Malta and its significance to Malta and the Maltese.

Sculpted wood Royal Cypher

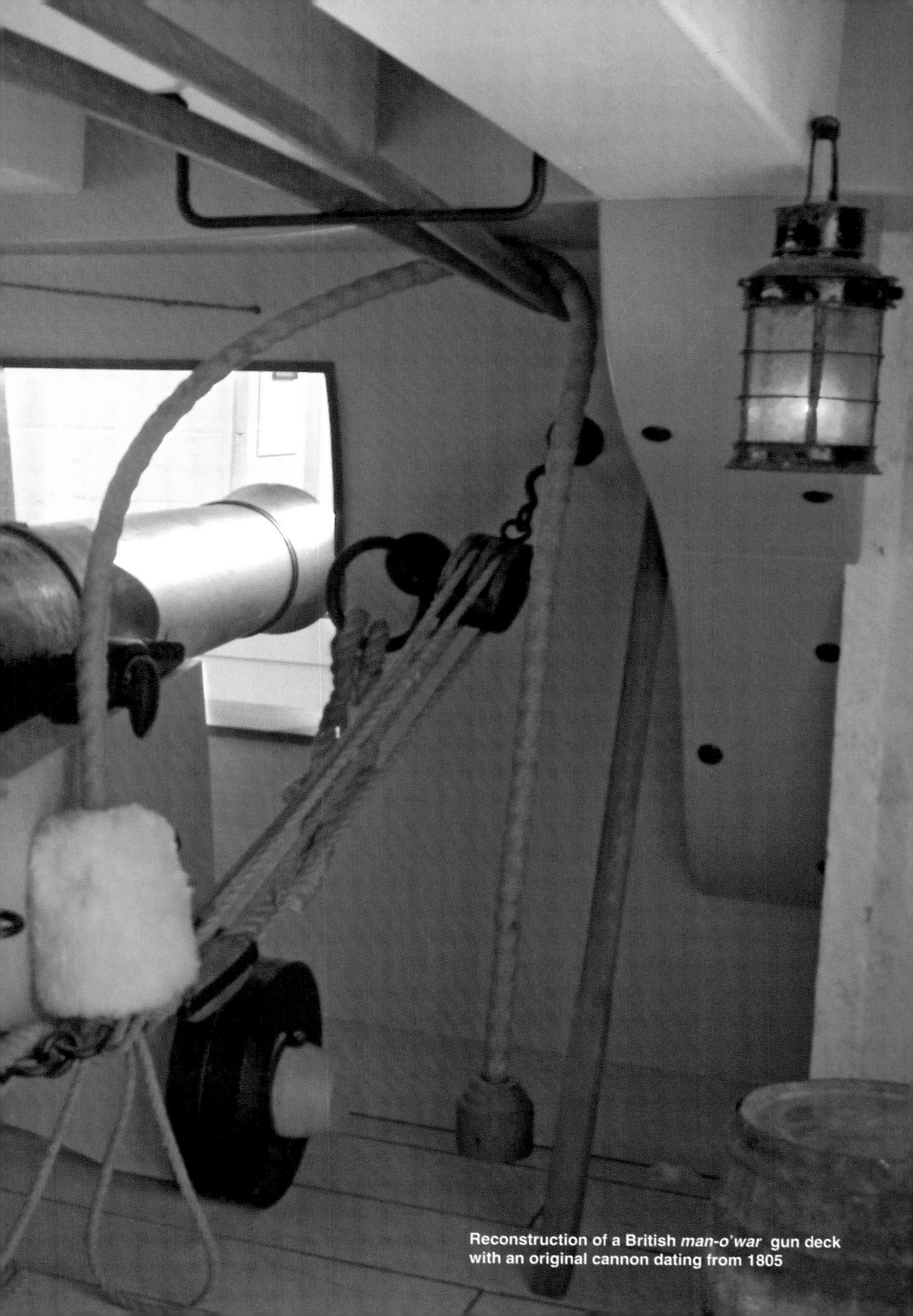

Reconstruction of a British *man-o'war* gun deck with an original cannon dating from 1805

Sir Alexander Ball, portrait by Gaetano Calleja

Nelson always insisted on a good medical service as the Royal Navy's backbone, which service was also extended to Malta with his efforts mainly in establishing a proper Naval Hospital. Nelson even earmarked *Villa Bichi* as the site for the Naval Hospital, the building of which commenced on this very site 25 years after his death at the Battle of Trafalgar. The naval medical services in Malta are best represented by the original architect's model of Bighi Naval Hospital,[20] datable to 1829. In the dockyard section, various tools and original dock patterns[21] are on display, as are foundry models and period photographs showing the construction of the various naval docks and of the breakwater. A 32'

Bust of Queen Victoria and general view of the British Naval Hall

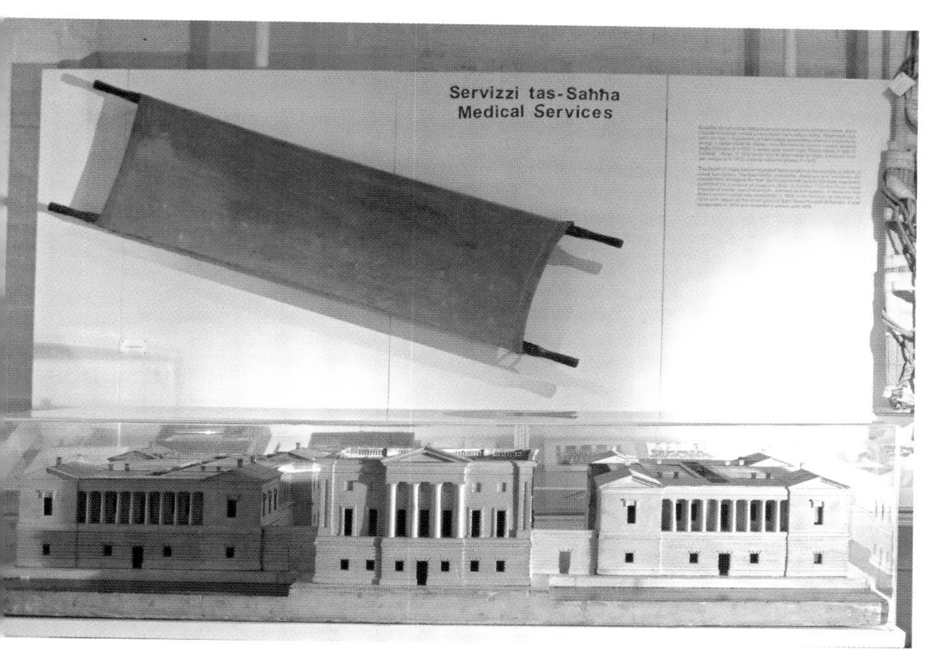

Architect's model of the Bighi Naval Hospital, donated by the National Maritime Museum of Greenwich

naval racing gig complete with oars delights water sports enthusiasts.

Law at sea during the early British period was taken seriously and steps were taken in order to stamp out crimes such as piracy. This legal aspect is represented by the Vice-Admiralty Court silver oar mace and seals and by several published books and documents treating piracy. This court was established in Malta in 1815 to deal with acts of piracy and its first President was the Governor of Malta Sir Thomas Maitland (1813-24). This court made legal history in Malta since it introduced trial by jury and was subsequently abolished by Imperial statutes of July 1860.

Above: Construction of the dockyard, *c.*1880s

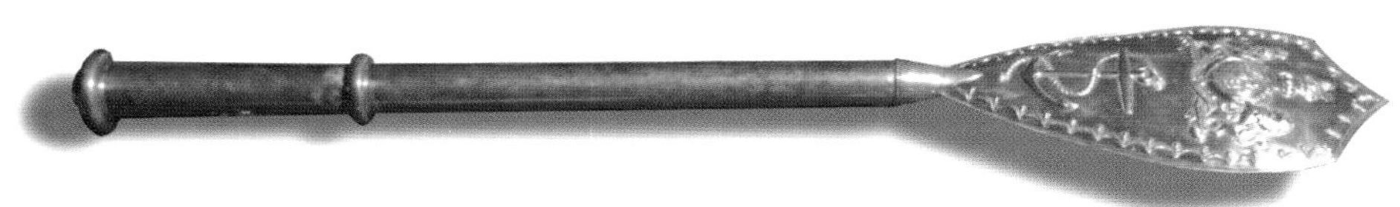

The Vice-Admirality Court silver oar mace

Right: The shop-front of the Eastney Canteen of Senglea, one of the several bars and food establishments catering for sailors, especially those of the Royal Navy

Bottom centre: Two late-20th-century Royal Navy ship models, made by Joseph Abela, keeper of models

A Victorian Royal Navy uniform

Jack Tar's life both at sea and on land is also given due attention. A sailor's kit, sailor-made souvenirs, ship models, and lithographs showing the life of a RN Mediterranean fleet sailor are exhibited. A reconstruction bar with artefacts coming from various bars popular with sailors around Malta is the main feature in this section. In a memorial for seamen and lost ships themselves, various brass, marble, and limestone headstones and memorials are exhibited. A token display illustrating disaster at sea tells the story of the sinking of HMS *Victoria* in 1893 in peaceful times with the loss of 358 men, including several Maltese ratings.

A small part of the museum's collection of uniforms is on display. These include parts from a mid-nineteenth-century Dockyard Battalion of Artillery uniform, once pertaining to Lt. T.P. Rickord. Victorian and Edwardian naval officers' uniforms and post-Second World War Dockyard Police, WRNS and RNA services uniforms. These uniforms, especially those dating to the Victorian period, show naval opulence at its best. They bring us

closer to personages who made British and Maltese history actually wearing them, as is the case with the uniforms of Admiral Sir Nigel Cecil, last British Forces commander in Malta recently presented to the Museum by Sir Nigel himself. Admiral Cecil actually wore all the said uniforms on particular occasions, which occasions were full of historical connections. One such uniform is the so-called 'No. 5', worn on 1 April 1979 on board HMS *London* when the ship left Malta at the closure of the British base which also officially brought to an end the Royal Navy's Mediterranean Fleet.

Royal Navy warship portraits and models dating from the late-eighteenth-century document the thrilling changes of ship construction and propulsion. A display of over 250 miniature models illustrate the evolution of the Royal Navy warships

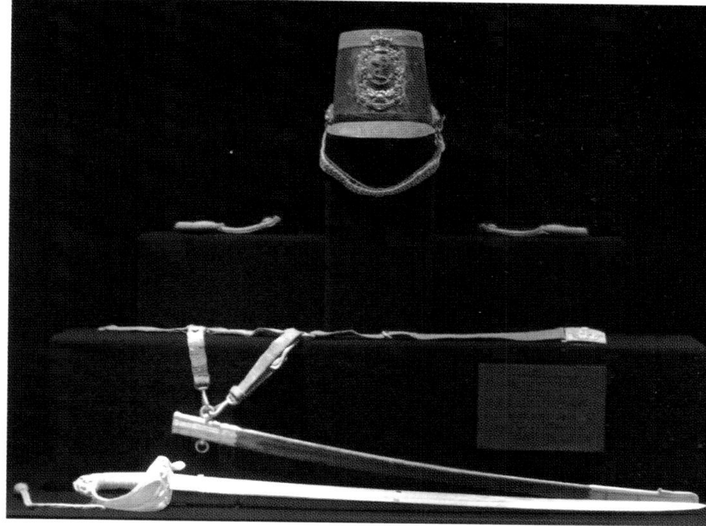

Surviving parts from the uniform of the Malta Dockyard Battalion

A post-Second World War Dockyard Police uniform

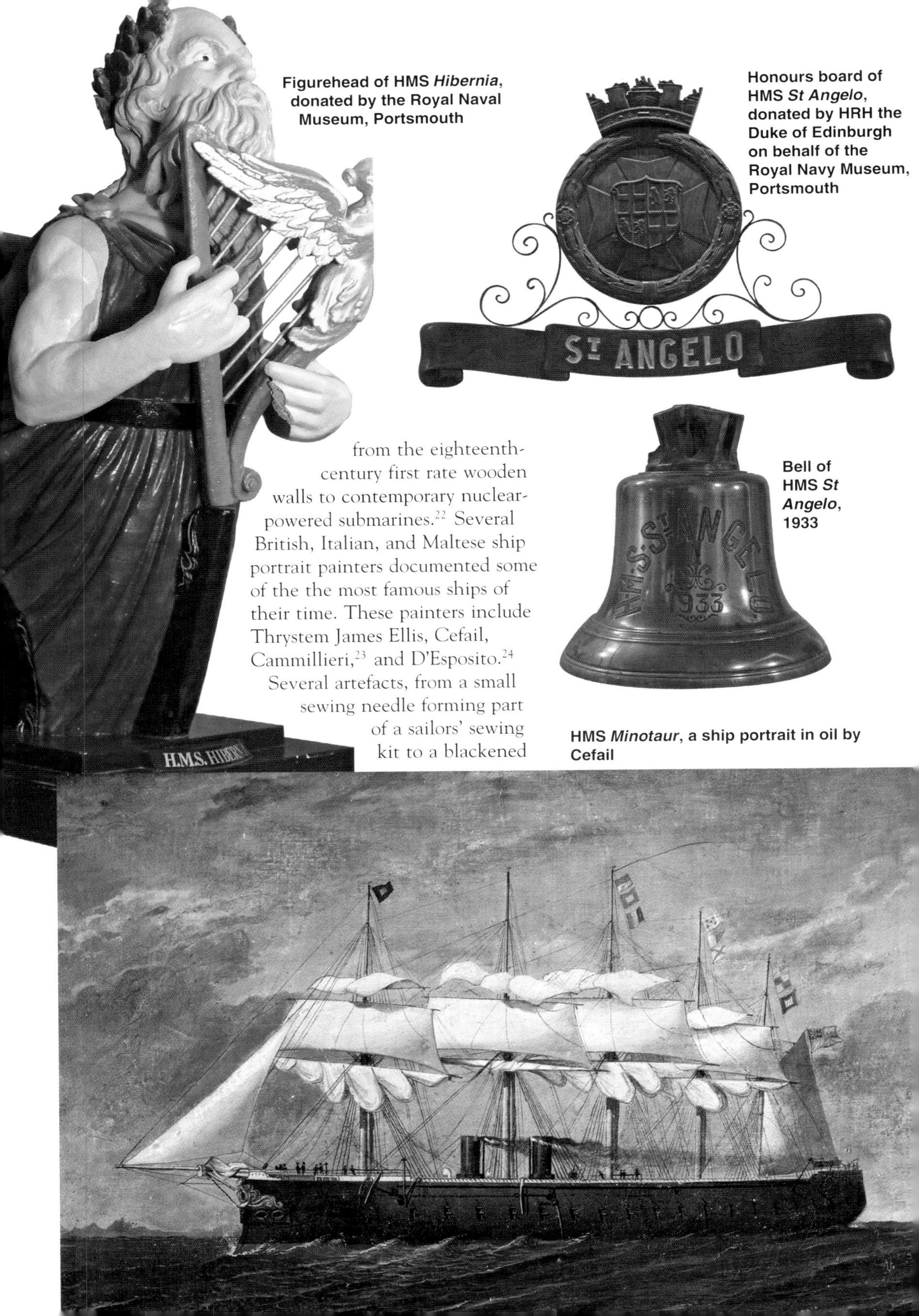

Figurehead of HMS *Hibernia*, donated by the Royal Naval Museum, Portsmouth

Honours board of HMS *St Angelo*, donated by HRH the Duke of Edinburgh on behalf of the Royal Navy Museum, Portsmouth

Bell of HMS *St Angelo*, 1933

from the eighteenth-century first rate wooden walls to contemporary nuclear-powered submarines.[22] Several British, Italian, and Maltese ship portrait painters documented some of the the most famous ships of their time. These painters include Thrystem James Ellis, Cefail, Cammillieri,[23] and D'Esposito.[24] Several artefacts, from a small sewing needle forming part of a sailors' sewing kit to a blackened

HMS *Minotaur*, a ship portrait in oil by Cefail

A canonade, late 18th century

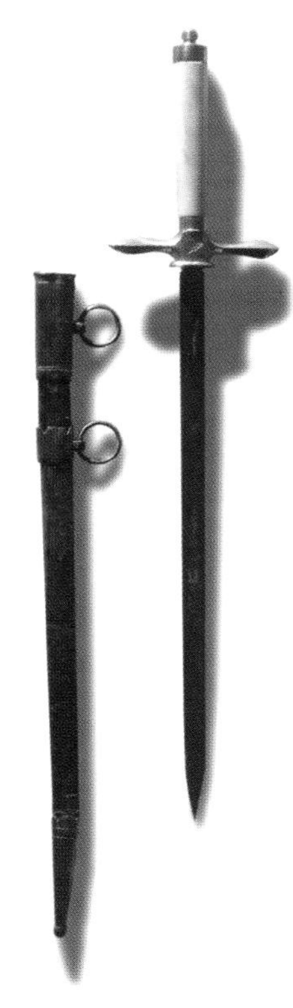

Left: A midshipman's dirk, *c.* 1775

smoking-pipe to the 3-ton figurehead of HMS *Hibernia* (1805),[25] are testimony to work ethics and past habits of sailors and of ship construction and equipment. Items which are testimony to particular epocs and eras include the Jolly Roger of HMS *Safari*, the bell and badge[26] of HMS *St Angelo*, several RN ship badges, nineteenth- and twentieth-century cane and rope fenders, a 1930s dinghy, a 1940s racing gig and trophies, souvenirs, and sailors handicrafts, mess plates, and NAAFI items.

British edged weapons, firearms, and guns belonging to various periods are also on display. A midshipman's dirk dating to c.1775 is the oldest British weapon on display. Several cutlasses, including some 'figure of eight' examples are also on exhibit. A sea-service pistol and various guns complete the section. Foremost in the gun collection is a prototype cannonade gun dating to the 1760s, a War Department British gun dating to the late seventeenth century, a Caron 24 pdr on carriage, and two 15 pdr naval RML guns.

Table setting with Royal Navy crockery

The *Ohio*, entering the Grand Harbour with much needed supplies on 15 August 1942

Right: The Jolly Roger of HMS *Safari*

Preceeding the final chapters of the Royal Navy in Malta is a section dedicated to Malta's role during the two World Wars.

During the First World War (1914-18), the Maltese islands were safe from aggression, with the Grand Harbour being the hub of the combined British and French fleets, assisted by a Japanese naval squadron and also as a Prisoner-of-War camp. The main role for Malta during the First World War was as a hospital base. Thousands of sick and wounded soldiers were nursed in Maltese hospitals which sprouted like mushrooms all over the island augmenting existing services hospitals, earning Malta the nickname of 'The Nurse of the Mediterranean'. Original material from the period on display include Maltese RN ratings medals and war silk souvenirs.

The scenario during the Second World War (1939-45) in Malta was quite different. Malta found itself

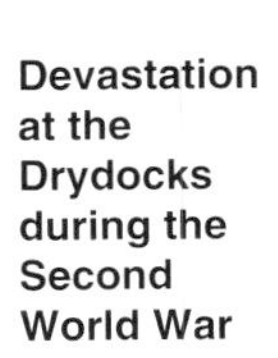

Devastation at the Drydocks during the Second World War

alone in the Mediterranean facing the Axis aerial bombings. During the blitz on HMS *Illustrious* in Grand Harbour in January 1941, almost the whole historic city of Senglea was destroyed. Materials, fuel, and food were running short by the end of 1941. The situation became desperate, and a shuttle of convoys from Alexandria and from England via Gibraltar were organized by the British. The most famous of these convoys was 'Operation Pedestal', nicknamed by the Maltese as *'Il-Konvoy ta' Santa Marija'*. On 15 August, 1942 the Texaco oil tanker *Ohio*, the only fuel tanker in the convoy, limped in a sinking condition into Grand Harbour, linched between two RN destroyers. The fuel brought in by *Ohio* was well used. Malta started to hit back at the Axis and more supplies could be brought in, thus saving the island. Malta from then on became to be known as 'The unsinkable aircraft carrier'. A model of the *Ohio* in war configuration is one of the star items in the Second World War section which features a host of period RN ship models and ship bells.

To mark the Royal Navy era in Malta are memorabilia such as the 'Commander British Forces Malta' life belt, Admiral Cecil's uniforms, documents, photographs, and the very last White Ensign to fly over Malta as an RN Base.

Royal Navy ships demaged beyond repair in the naval docks at Malta

Admiral Cecil, the Mediterranean Fleet's last Admiral with the Admiral's barge and HMS *St Angelo* as a backgorund

Early 20th-century navigational aids and chart

Bottom right: Various navigational instruments from the 16th to the 18th century

The Nocturnal, dated 1574

The museum possesses a small but important collection of navigation instruments with items dating from the sixteenth century. An exceptional complete Nocturnal dated 1574 is the centrepiece of this collection together with Maltese-made navigation instruments. Also displayed are an eighteenth-century manuscript portolan and a parchment sea chart together with other eighteenth- and nineteenth-century printed *portolans* and sea charts.

An important section is that devoted to communication at sea between the ships themselves and land. The exhibits include various original eighteenth-century manuscript signalling manuals with various small illustrations pertaining to both the galley and the third rate squadrons of the Order of St John. Some nineteenth-century printed manuals, mostly pertaining to the Royal Navy, are also included in this section. Pride of place amongst these manuals is taken by the manuscript and illuminated signalling manual dated 1700 issued under the command of Fra Gio. Batta Spinola, who was elected Captain General of the Galleys in the same year.

Sky and stars observation and calculations were not only restricted to ships at sea and to the Order's Nautical School. The

Far left: Portrait of an unidentified Maltese pilot, late 17th-century

Bottom left: Portrait of a 19th-century Maltese navigator

Left: Various 19th-century navigational instruments

Order was keen for academic study related to the subject in question, prompting the installation in 1783 of an astronomical observatory at the Grand Master's Palace at Valletta on the advice of Deodat de Dolomieu, the Order's best-known scientist. The observatory was located in what is known as the Palace *turretta* – the tower. An astronomer, Jean-Auguste d'Angos, was hired for the post but later proved not to be up to the desired standards. Unfortunately, all the equipment was lost during a fire on 13 March 1789, together with all records and documentation.[27] The tower in question today serves a maritime purpose. Commanding a clear view of Malta's two large harbours on either side of Valletta, it is still referred to as the *turretta* and functions as a communication platform assisting small and large craft coming in and out of the Grand and Marsamxett harbours.

Below: Signalling orders of Fra Gio. Batta Spinola, Captain General of the Galleys, 1700

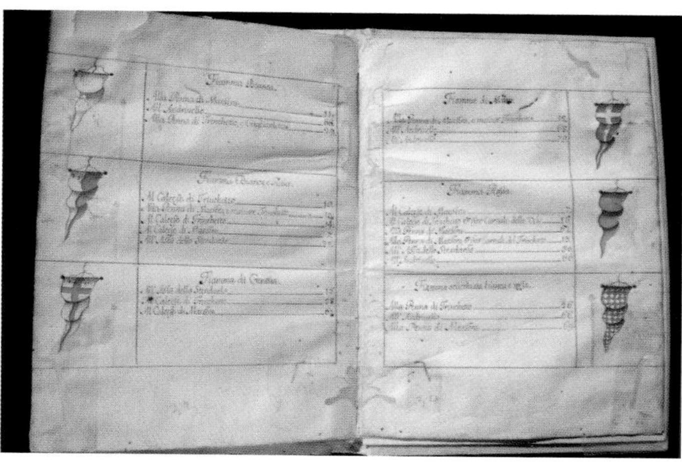

Bottom: An 18th-century signalling code book pertaining to the navy of the Order of St John

The Customs Hall, showing the customs bell and official scales dating from the mid-19th century

The Maltese Customs played and still play a vital role in Maltese maritime affairs. More than 90 per cent of Malta's imports and exports, to this date, are still via the sea. The story of the Malta Customs is told through original artefacts that pertained to this institution. The official standard weights and measures used by the Maltese Customs are on exhibit, the oldest of which date to the early eighteenth century with the coat-of-arms of Grand Master Vilhena (1722-36). Any weights and measures which were to be used in the Maltese

Seals of Malta Customs, 1800 and 1815

Various types of wieights and measures used by the Customs in the 18th century

islands had to be calibrated with these very official standard weights and measures, all appropriately marked with successive grand masters' marks.

Cereal wooden measures, brass and copper liquid measures, passports, bills of lading, and the one-off official Customs seals are on display. Other official weights and measures belong to the British period. An exceptional item belonging to this period is the Michelangelo Sapiano scales, reputed to have been able to weigh even a single grain.

In the same hall is a small display about the Marine Police. This autonomous police unit was amalgamated with the Malta Police in the early twentieth century. Artefacts include a uniform of the Marine Police Corp and a pre-Second World War life buoy marked 'Malta Police'.

TRADITIONAL MALTESE BOATS

Maltese traditional boat models, tools, and paintings constitute the basis of a small hall dedicated to the colourful Maltese boats. The Museum possesses a collection of over forty full-scale traditional Maltese boats, which presently cannot be displayed owing to lack of restored spaces. These period models, themselves excellent exhibits, fill in the gap for the time being.

These models tell the story of each type of Maltese traditional boat, its use and purpose, such as the *kajjik* and the *fregatina* and the actual evolution of specific types, such as the *dgħajsa*. Nearly extinct boat types are also on exhibit such as *tal-Latini* and the *ferilla*, as are the now more important models of extinct boat types, such as the *speronara* and the governor's *gondla*.

Some specimen decorative sculpted components of the Maltese traditional *dgħajsa* are on exhibit. These include various examples of *makrunetti* and *spallieri*. The former, which are the ends of decorative wash boards, are mostly always carved as crouching lions. The latter, which are the backrests, mostly have a centrally-glazed roundel in which either Brittania, St George, or an HM ship badge was placed, showing the pro-British sentiments of the Maltese '*diso*' man.[28]

A variety of boat – and ship – building tools are exhibited together with a whole set of master moulds for the building of a traditional Maltese *fregatina*. The tools on exhibit include master-shipwright-made tools; these took pride in incising the metal parts and sculpting the wooden handles and other parts of their tools.

Exhibited alongside these models are some *ex-voto* paintings which tell the story of the Maltese mariner's faith and devotion towards God, the Virgin Mary under various titles, and various saints. Fear and peril are well illustrated, as is the credence

A model of a *Speronara*

Ex-voto painting invoking the intercession of St Joseph showing a *ferilla* in a storm

in Divine intervention in such moments. Many Maltese mariners commissioned the *ex-voto tabelle* to be displayed in specific shrines as thanksgiving.

At times, Maltese sailors incised the images of their boats and ships onto the exterior walls of these shrines, especially those of a Marian devotion. Most probably, this was a tangible sign that their boat or ship was placed under the protection of the Virgin Mary under a specific title or a saint venerated at that particular shrine. Some graffiti plaster copies of the original works are included in this section.

A graffito of a sailing ship

MODELS OF TRADITIONAL MALTESE BOATS

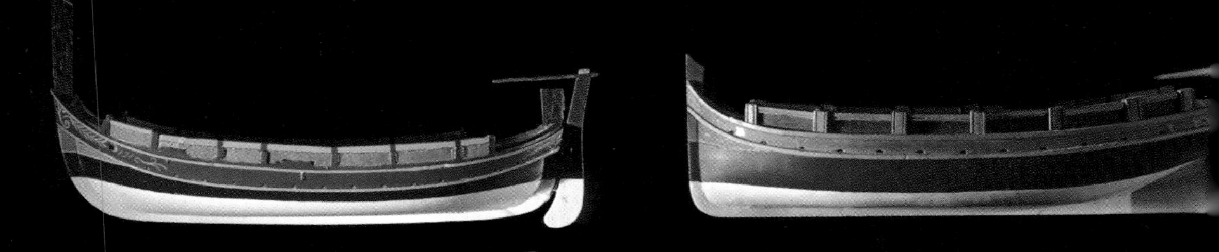

Ferilla

Kajjik

Sailing ferilla

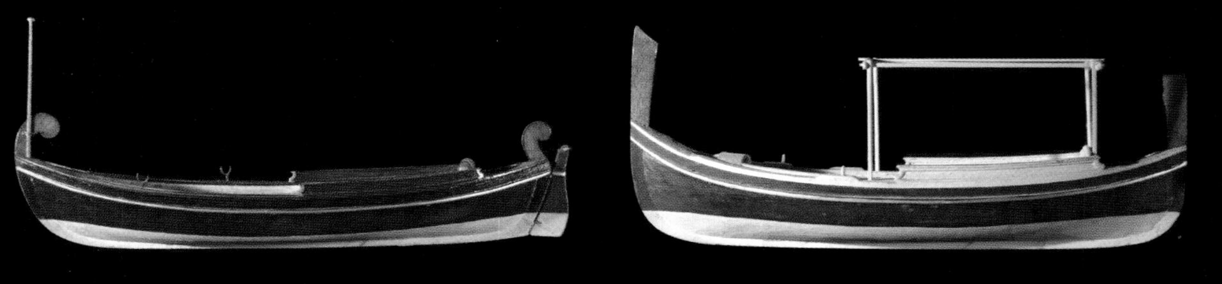

Gondla

Dockyard-type dgħajsa

Latin-rigged Gozo boat

MERCANTILE MARINE

Presently, only a token display of mercantile marine items features in the Museum. The present display focuses mainly on the merchant ship-building activity in Malta mainly up to the mid-nineteenth century. Half-models of some of the Maltese-built merchant ships are displayed, together with several other foreign merchant ship models and a few ship portraits, all with a Maltese connection.

Prominent Maltese ship-building families such as the German from Senglea, the Mirabitur from Vittoriosa, and the Camilleri from Cospicua made a name in constructing sturdy merchant ships. These ship-building firms are represented by the half-models of the German-built merchant ships *Maria Concetta* and the *German Brothers* dating from the 1840s.[29] These models were built with the plank on frame method, unlike the rest of the half-models on exhibit, which are solid built. Another important half-model dated 1882 is that of the Newcastle-upon-Tyne-built merchant ship SS *Tagliaferro*, built for the Maltese shipping company Biagio Tagliaferro.[30] Other half-models represent smaller craft of British origin as adapted by Maltese boat-builders. These include the ketch or *qicc* and two different-sized launches or *laneċ*. An important collection of traditional Maltese boats' half-models is also on display. These include the 'bread-and-butter' type models of the *dgħajsa tal-pass*, the *fregatina*, and the *kajjik*.

The *Sant'Antonio* block-built model is the most naïve model on

General view of the Mercantile history section

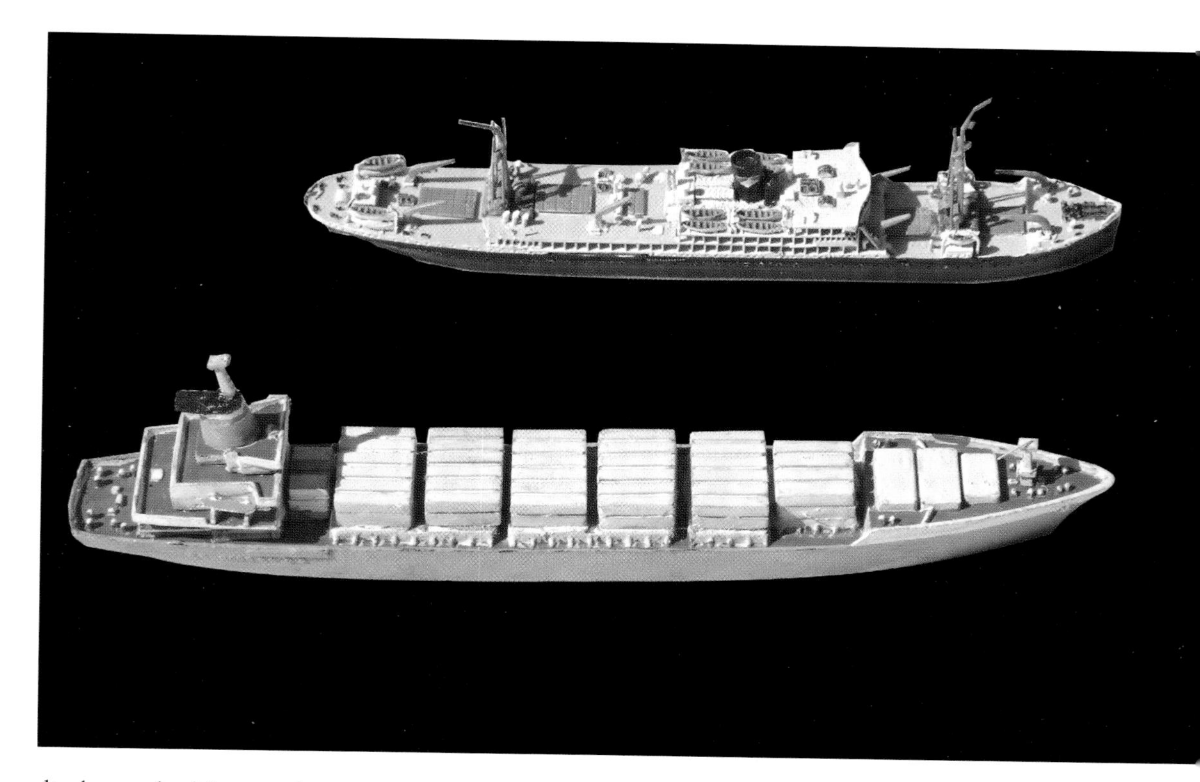

Mercantile ship models

display at the Museum; however, the very fact that it was built by its own master merits its display. This merchant brig schooner model illustrates a type of merchant ship which has since vanished from our seas. Another model is that of the Italian wine brig schooner *Grigale*, which was a regular visitor to Malta ferrying wine from Sicily. A large historic contemporary model of the Austro-Hungarian merchant barque *Costantino*, another then frequent visitor to Malta, features prominently in this representative section.[31]

Amongst the displayed nineteenth-century and early twentieth-century merchant ship portraits are those of the Malta-based Gollcher fleet of sail and steam ships, namely the *L'Isle Adam* and the *Gleneagles*.[32] The Museum possesses a large collection of early nineteenth-century ship portraits by Nicholas Camilleri or Cammillieri, an acclaimed Maltese ship-portrait painter. Most of the ship portraits with a Maltese content have as a background the entrance to the Grand Harbour. Maltese, British, and other foreign ships were portrayed in this way, as was the Greek merchant ship *Deo Adelphi*, yet another frequent visitor, leaving the Grand Harbour in 1870.[33]

Studies to complete the layout of a 600 sq.m. hall designated to receive the mercantile marine and customs collections are under way. Several merchant ship models have been restored and others lie waiting for their turn, as are ship portrait paintings, several artefacts, and various documents. The artefacts will tell the story of the Maltese and foreign merchants who used Maltese ports and made use of the Maltese Customs from the Order's period to the present day.

MARINE ENGINEERING

The Marine Engineering Hall is housed on two levels. At the lower level, the working triple-expansion steam engine and auxiliary engines of the 1952-built grab hopper dragger *Anadrian* are displayed.[34] Other items pertaining to the ship are on display, including the engine-room tools, spare parts, documents, the ship's model, and a reconstruction of the captain's cabin equipped with all the original navigation and control systems. The *Anadrian* made Maltese history since, when it was brought over as new in 1954, it started clearing Maltese harbours from wartime debris and other silt accumulated since the late 1930s. After a long working life, it was condemned in 1989 but since it was government-owned, the Malta Maritime Museum was quick in securing all the engines and other items, knowing well how rare such an opportunity was. The meticulous dismantling of the vessel's items and their restoration took almost twelve years, in which time the hall was also restored.

In the upper level, a selection of small inboard engines dating from 1923 and various outboard engines dating from the 1950s are found. The story of the propeller is told aided by various bronze propellers dating from the mid-nineteenth century. Marine engineers testing equipment together with reference books and various other marine engineering related models can be admired at this level. Five working scaled models of steam engines made by dockyard apprentices document the skills and abilities of these apprentices. These pieces were usually made as their course test pieces.

The reconstructed *Anadrian* wheel house

General view of the lower Anadrian Hall, containing all steam engines and tools of the ship

The upper level of the Anadrian Hall containing a collection of inboard and outboard engines

Model of the *Anadrian*

REFERENCE LIBRARY

The reference library in use by Svetlik Agius, full-scale boat technician

The specifically maritime-oriented reference library is the backbone of researchers, both museum staff and external. Apart from around 3,000 published books, the Museum also subscribes to some of the world's best maritime journals, such as the British *Mariner's Mirror*, *The American Neptune*, and the French *Neptunia*. A specific section is reserved for rare books and archival material. Also preserved in the library is the collection of over 6,000 maritime-related photographs. Another small collection is that of maritime-related audio-visual material.

RESTORATION LAB AND WORKSHOPS

A ship and boat models restoration laboratory is housed within the Museum. Almost all of the Museum's models on exhibit had to be restored prior to being exhibited. Some of the most problematic restoration projects were made on the core Order of St John period (1530-1798) models, especially on the large Nautical School model. Other models which tested the ability of the restorers were a bone, brass, and wood clipper model and a French Napoleonic prisoner-of-war wood model. This latter model's

Joseph Abela (Heritage Malta keeper of the models) restoring a contemporary model of HMS *Hood*

masts, spars, and rigging were virtually in a hopeless state before restoration; however, with research, skill, and lots of patience on the restorers' part, such models have been brought back to their pristine condition.

The laboratory also houses a model-making workshop which produces various models of contemporary boats and ships that made Maltese maritime history in some way or another. These models include a Roman grain transport ship, the extinct traditional Maltese passenger- and cargo-boat type known as the *speronara*, HMS *Dainty*, the grab hopper dragger *Anadrian*, the ferry *Għawdex*,[35] all produced by the keeper of models and various Armed Forces of Malta Maritime Squadrons patrol boats made by the model maker.

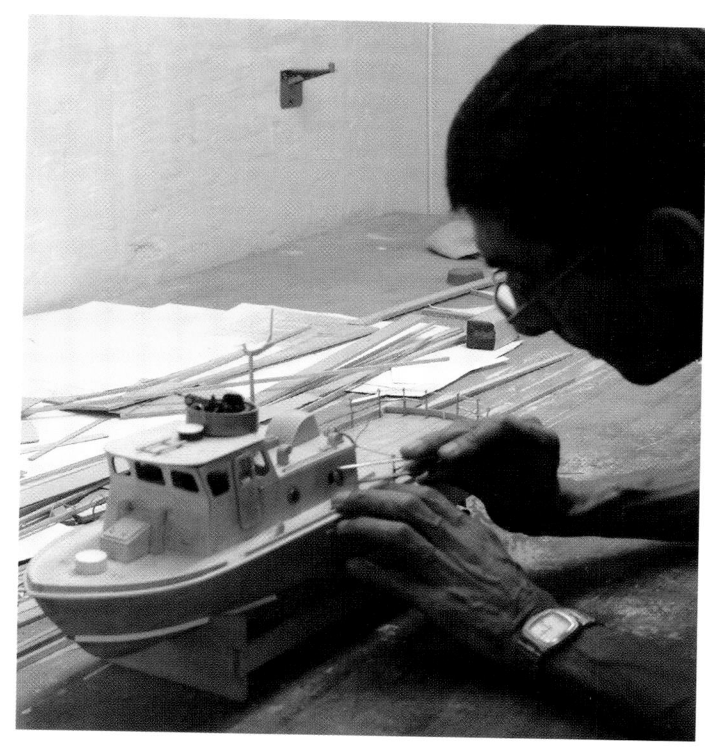

Emmanuel Gatt, model maker, at work on the model of the Swift Class patrol boat

RESERVE COLLECTION

The Museum's reserve collection contains items which are preserved pending the development of further halls and sections. Other items are conserved as duplicates of those items on exhibit for reference and study purposes. It is earnestly hoped that restoration works at the Malta Maritime Museum will be concluded within ten years, so that the various proposed thematic and chronological halls will be opened to the public.

Some unusual items are preserved in the reserve collection. Nelson's bed, said to have been used in Naples, is one such item. Brought by the Royal Navy from Naples in 1943 as a trophy, it was handed over from one admiral to another until 1979 when it was donated to the Maltese government. An antique traditional Maltese boat model with trial inboard engine fittings is one of the small treasures preserved in the reserve collection. A somewhat unsightly item is a placenta conserved in spirit, known in naval jargon as 'a sailor's cawl'. The 'sailor's cawl' was given to a sailor by his wife after a successful childbirth as a good luck talisman as was customary up to the Second World War with sailors.

Model of MV *Għawdex*

St Angelo Hall, a multi-purpose hall used for temporary exhibitions

MUSEUM FACILITIES

The museum is equipped with a function hall ideal for various activities. Patrons of the museum's functions hall include the President and Prime Minister of Malta, various Ministers, Ambassadors, High Commissioners, the University of Malta, and corporate bodies. An audiovisual theatre seating up to 180 persons is planned, as is a cafeteria with 200 covers. A museum shop will complete the services offered by the Museum.

EXHIBITIONS

As from December 2000, a small monthly exhibition has been put up with those items that are normally preserved in the reserve collection or in the library. On a yearly basis, generally in December, the exhibition is devoted to recent acquisitions. Featured titles included the Pedestal Convoy, a sailor's ditty box, nineteenth-century log books, and US Navy memorabilia.

NOTES

1. The first chairman of the committee was Judge Stephen Borg Cardona who, after his demise, was succeeded by Prof. Anthony Bonanno. Mr Joseph Muscat was the secretary and also the principal consultant on the novel project. Mr Antonio Espinosa Rodriguez, then curator Fine Arts Museum, was appointed as the first curator of the Malta Maritime Museum and acted as the committee's executive.
2. Joseph Muscat, 'The Arsenal' in Lino Bugeja et al (eds.), *Birgu – a Maltese Maritime City* (Malta, 1993), 260.
3. Ibid.
4. Ibid.
5. Joseph Muscat, *The Birgu Galley Arsenal* (Malta, 2001), 6.
6. Ibid. and Muscat, 'The Arsenal', 260.
7. The original plan is at Kew Records Office, England. A copy is at the Malta Maritime Museum. This plan, together with others related with the Naval Bakery, was found during research conducted by David Drago at Kew.
8. *Malta Mail*, 11 April 1845, 2. The first biscuits were offered to the governor, the admiral superintendent, and their guests.
9. Moira Bishop, 'Victorian Bread Ovens at Vittoriosa', 1994. Unpublished study presented to the Malta Maritime Museum.
10. Ibid. and R.D. Ridding, 'Ship's Biscuits (Hard Tack) – Historical Notes And Recipe', Undated study at the Malta Maritime Museum.
11. G.A. Flatters and Les Kirk, 2004, Correspondence with the writer re the Bakery's clock.
12. The Dutton family, starting from the father William and his two sons, Matthew and Thomas, were renowned for clocks, watches, chronometers, etc. Matthew was best known for domestic clocks and, since the style of the clock is very similar to those produced by Thwaites and Reed of London, the clock was possibly supplied by them with some modifications made by Matthew Dutton, hence his maker's plate. Thwaites and Reed produced, amongst other clocks, the Big Ben clock movements in St Stephen's Tower in the House of Parliament in Westminster, London.
13. Possibly these renowned Maltese clock and watch-makers from Vittoriosa were either the actual local clock suppliers in the 1890s or had restored the clock movements sometime in the 19th century.
14. Ibid.
15. Some items have already been donated by the AFM, Maritime squadron.
16. Donated by the Greek Hellenic Maritime Museum through the Hon. Consul of Malta in Athens.
17. On loan from Dr Alexander Cachia Zammit.
18. Verbal communication with Mr Joseph Muscat.
19. Includes the Blockade period.
20. This model was donated by the National Maritime Museum, Greenwich in 1993.
21. These models and various other items in this section were donated by the then Malta Drydocks Corporation, now Malta Shipyards.
22. These models together with an equal amout of naval and merchant ship models were donated by Col. R.J. McGarel Groves, RM (Rt) between 2001 and 2004.
23. Four Camilleri ship portraits were donated by Mid-Med Bank Ltd, now HSBC in 1994.
24. One of the several D'Esposito ship portrait paintings was donated by Dr Alexander Cachia Zammit in 1991.
25. The figurehead was donated by Portsmouth Naval Museum in 1994.
26. This badge was donated to the museum by H.R.H. the Duke of Edinburgh in 1992, who was also instrumental in HMS *Hibernia* donation.
27. Giovanni Bonello,'The Grand Masters' Palace In The Making' in *Histories of Malta, Versions and Diversions*, (Malta, 2002), p183-4.
28. The word 'diso' was used as Naval jargon referring to the *barklori* or rowers of the traditional Maltese *dgħajsa*.
29. These two half models were donated by Fr German, a descendant of the ship builders in 1992.
30. This half model was donated by Bank of Valletta Ltd in 1995.
31. This model is on permanent loan from the Malta Maritime Authority.
32. These and two other ship portraits were donated by O.F. Gollcher & Sons Ltd in 1994.
33. This ship portrait was donated by Lombard Bank in 1996.
34. These engines were taken out of the vessel with the assistance of Cassar Ship Repair Yard of Marsa.
35. This model was sponsored by Gozo Channel Company Ltd.

FRIENDS OF THE MALTA MARITIME MUSEUM

The 'Friends' was set up in 1993 as an independent group of maritime history enthusiasts who help in various ways the Malta Maritime Museum. Some members actually lend themselves assisting in the Museum's photographic archive, the library in general, and in specific research projects. Other 'friends' help in cleaning or renovating items. From time to time, the 'Friends' donate artefacts to the Museum purchased from the 'Friends' own funds.

The marble Salvago arsenal memorial, 1654

ERICH VON MANSTEIN

LEADERSHIP ▪ STRATEGY ▪ CONFLICT

ROBERT FORCZYK

First published in Great Britain in 2010 by Osprey Publishing,
PO Box 883, Oxford, OX1 9PL, UK
PO Box 3985, New York, NY 10185-3985, USA
Email: info@ospreypublishing.com

Osprey Publishing, part of Bloomsbury Publishing Plc

Transferred to digital print on demand 2015.

First published 2010
1st impression 2010

Printed and bound by PrintOnDemand-Worldwide.com, Peterborough, UK.

A CIP catalogue record for this book is available from the British Library.

ISBN: 978 1 84603 465 7

Editorial by Ilios Publishing Ltd, Oxford, UK (www.iliospublishing.com)
Page layout by Myriam Bell Design, France
Index by Margaret Vaudrey
Typeset in 1 Stone Serif and Officina Sans ITC Standard
Maps by Mapping Specialists Ltd
Originated by PPS Grasmere Ltd, Leeds, UK

Artist's note
Readers may care to note that the original paintings from which the colour plates in this book were prepared are available for private sale. The Publishers retain all reproduction copyright whatsoever. All enquiries should be addressed to:

Scorpio, 158 Mill Road, Hailsham, East Sussex BN27 2SH, UK
Email: scorpiopaintings@btinternet.com

The Publishers regret that they can enter into no correspondence upon this matter.

Acknowledgements
I wish to thank Nik Cornish, Monika Geilen (Bundesarchiv), Ralph Gibson (Novosti) and HITM Archives for their help with this project.

Dedication
This volume is dedicated to SSG Collin J. Bowen, 1-175 IN, 29 ID (LT), MD-ARNG; died 14 March 2008 from wounds received in Afghanistan.

The Woodland Trust
Osprey Publishing are supporting the Woodland Trust, the UK's leading woodland conservation charity, by funding the dedication of trees.

www.ospreypublishing.com

CONTENTS

INTRODUCTION

From the 17th century, the Prussian Army developed a tradition of *Bewegungskrieg* (manoeuvre warfare), which was gradually refined by the creation of the Großer Generalstab (Great General Staff) in the 19th century. Due to the necessity of having to fight enemies on multiple fronts and often outnumbered, Prussian doctrine favoured the use of bold operational manoeuvring to put the enemy in a position of disadvantage and to seek a rapid conclusion to campaigns in a decisive battle before the enemy's superior numbers could be brought to bear. Prussian armies demonstrated a great talent for *Bewegungskrieg* during the Austro-Prussian War of 1866 and the Franco-Prussian War of 1870–71, where they succeeded in outmanoeuvring and defeating strong opponents in lightning campaigns. Imperial Germany carried this tradition into World War I and its Schlieffen Plan tried to use rapid manoeuvre to knock France out of the war in a matter of weeks. However, this time *Bewegungskrieg* failed to achieve a knock-out blow in the first round and Germany was forced to fight a *Stellungskrieg* (war of position) in the trenches, which resulted in her armies being ground down by four years of attritional combat. One participant who learned his trade as a young staff officer in this war was Erich von Manstein, who would later become one of the most successful exponents and practitioners of manoeuvre warfare in the next global conflict.

Erich von Manstein in 1895, age 8. (Author's collection)

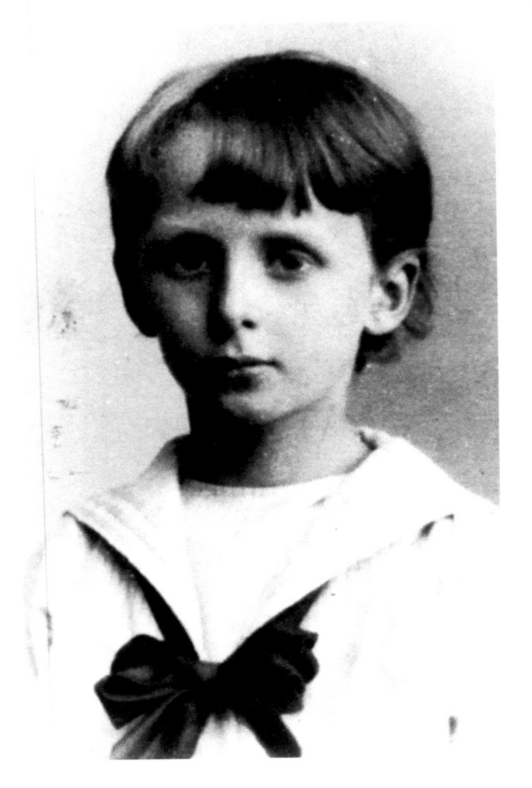

Manstein believed in the Prussian traditions of *Bewegungskrieg* as an article of faith and his operational genius lay in the ease with which he was able to impose simple solutions upon complex military problems. During World War II, Manstein used his talent for manoeuvre warfare to make vital contributions to the Third Reich's war effort. First, he conceived the *Sichelschnitt* plan that enabled German armies to defeat

France in just six weeks. Second, he conquered the Crimea and virtually annihilated four Soviet armies in the process. Third, he helped to prevent a complete collapse of the German southern front in the disastrous winter of 1942–43 and mounted a skilful counteroffensive that regained the operational initiative. Later when the war in the east turned against Germany, Manstein advocated a mobile defence as the best means of avoiding costly *Stellungskrieg* and gradually wearing down the enemy.

In addition to being an apostle of manoeuvre warfare in both offensive and defensive situations, Manstein was a tactical innovator who sought means to increase the battlefield effectiveness of his troops. Prior to the war, he recommended the development of *Sturmartellerie* units. During the war, he daringly used assault boats to outflank tactical obstacles and experimented with novel formations, such as an artillery division and a heavy Panzer regiment – both of which were very successful.

Cadet Manstein, age 15, in his last year at the Kadettenanstalt in Plön in 1902. (Author's collection)

However, Manstein's style of warfare gradually became less applicable as Germany's resources were exhausted in six years of bitter warfare. As the tide of war turned against Germany, Hitler forced German armies to defend territorial objectives that he regarded as critical for either political or economic resources, but which effectively tethered his commanders. Unable to conduct true *Bewegungskrieg*, Manstein was reduced to trading space for time. After the war, Manstein was one of the first German commanders to write his memoirs, which he used to develop his reputation as 'Hitler's most brilliant general'. In fact, Manstein's skills were not unique and the Wehrmacht had other skilled practitioners of *Bewegungskrieg*. Yet there is little doubt that Manstein was one of the most ardent exponents of manoeuvre warfare in World War II and his campaigns marked the apogee of the Wehrmacht's operational art.

THE EARLY YEARS, 1887–1913

The future field marshal was born in Braunfels in Hesse on 24 November 1887. His father was a Prussian artillery officer, Generalleutnant Eduard von Lewinski (1829–1906) and his mother was Helene von Sperling (1847–1910). Erich was the couple's tenth child and Helene had made an arrangement with her sister Hedwig and her husband, Oberst Georg von Manstein (1844–1913), to allow them to raise their newborn, since they had no sons to carry the family name.

The Preußische Hauptkadettenanstalt (higher cadet academy) at Gross Lichterfelde, where Manstein received his military education from 1902 to 1906. (Author's collection)

Between the Lewinskis, Sperlings and Mansteins, Erich was related to no fewer than five Prussian generals and he was immersed in Prussian military traditions from the very beginning. Both of Erich's grandfathers had been generals and one of them, General Albrecht von Manstein, had led IX Armeekorps during the Franco-Prussian War. One of his mother's sisters, Gertrud, married Paul von Hindenburg, which made the future *Generalfeldmarschall* and president of Germany Erich's uncle.

Erich began his formal education at the age of seven, attending the Lycée in Strasburg where he spent the next five years. In 1900, the 13-year-old Erich was sent to the Kadettenanstalt (cadet school) at Plön in Schleswig-Holstein. During this period, Erich was also enrolled in the Corps of Pages, which required him to serve in Kaiser Wilhelm's court during the winter breaks. He apparently enjoyed his service as a page quite a bit, since he mentioned it more extensively in his memoirs than his service in World War I.

In 1902, Erich went to the Preußische Hauptkadettenanstalt (higher cadet academy) at Gross Lichterfelde in the south-west suburbs of Berlin, which was the primary training centre for Prussian officers. On 6 March 1906 he was commissioned as a *Fähnrich* (ensign) in the infantry. He then attended the Königliche Kriegsschule (royal military academy) at Schloss Engers on the Rhine, near Koblenz, for further training.

As a freshly minted infantry officer, Manstein was posted to the 3. Garde-Regiment zu Fuß, which was Hindenburg's old regiment. This regiment was regarded as a parade unit and a place for noblemen to earn military decorations. Erich served in the regiment as a junior officer for eight years. In 1913, the regiment sent him to attend the Kriegsakademie, which put him on a possible path to the prestigious Großer Generalstab. However, before Manstein could complete the course, a crisis in the Balkans escalated into a major European conflict.

Leutnant Erich von Manstein in the formal dress uniform of the 3. Garde-Regiment zu Fuß, June 1907. (Author's collection)

THE MILITARY LIFE, 1914–43

World War I, 1914–18

When World War I began in August 1914, Leutnant von Manstein was assigned as adjutant of the 2. Garde-Reserve-Regiment and served initially in Belgium but was then transferred with his unit to East Prussia, which gave Manstein his first taste of action against the Russians. Manstein was involved in the advance towards Warsaw in October 1914 before Russian counterattacks forced the outnumbered German forces to retreat. During the withdrawal, Manstein was wounded near Kattowice, west of Krakow. After recovering in Wiesbaden for six months, he returned in 1915 to serve as a junior staff officer first in Poland, then in Serbia. For his performance during the Serbian Campaign, Manstein was awarded the Eisernes Kreuz 1. Klasse (Iron Cross, 1st Class). Afterwards, Manstein was transferred back to France in April 1916, where he served as a staff officer in the Verdun sector and then later on the Somme sector. Although he had not been trained as a Generalstab officer, in October 1917 Manstein was made a division-level Ia (operations) officer and he spent the rest of the war in that role.

Although he was an infantry officer, Manstein held no troop commands during the entire war, which was rather odd for a company-grade officer. Furthermore, most of his staff assignments were of a very secondary nature until very late in the war. Compared to those of his peers who survived and went on to become senior officers in the Wehrmacht, it was not exactly a brilliant war career but Manstein did achieve recognition as a skilled and diligent staff officer, which ensured his inclusion in the post-war Reichswehr.

Hauptmann von Manstein in late 1915, while he was serving as an adjutant in 10. Armee in northern Poland. (Author's collection)

Service in the Reichswehr, 1919–35

Once the Armistice was signed and revolutionary turmoil broke out in Berlin, the Imperial Army began to disintegrate and Manstein found himself involved in the process of trying to salvage useful fragments from the chaos. Manstein was sent to Breslau in February 1919 to work with General der Infanterie 'Fritz' von Loßberg in organizing the post-war Reichswehr, which was limited to only 100,000 men under the terms of the Treaty of Versailles. Loßberg was a gifted Generalstab officer and he soon became one of Manstein's best mentors.

During his New Year's holiday in January 1920, the 32-year-old Manstein returned to Silesia where he met Jutta Sybille von Loesch, who was 19. He abruptly proposed three days later and they were married on 10 June 1920. Jutta was from a very wealthy aristocratic family in Silesia who lived only 2km (1 mile) from the new border with Poland and who consequently had lost

Hauptmann Erich von Manstein (on horseback) with his 6. Kompanie, Infanterie-Regiment 5, on a training march in 1923. He normally spent three days a week on training marches and one day at the firing range. (Author's collection)

much of their land due to the Treaty of Versailles. Manstein settled into married life and a daughter, Gisela, was born in April 1921.

In October 1921 – after 15 years in the infantry – Manstein was finally given his first troop assignment: command of 6. Kompanie of Infanterie-Regiment 5 in Angermünde, north-east of Berlin. While he was at Angermünde, his first son, Gero, was born in December 1922.

After two years as a company commander, Manstein returned to staff duties. Since the Treaty of Versailles had stripped Germany of its Generalstab and forced the closure of its Kriegsakademie, the Reichswehr sought to evade these restrictions by training a new group of professional German officers in small study groups. Manstein was one of the lucky few who were brought into these groups and this became a critical period in the development of his military concepts. Generaloberst Hans von Seeckt directed Reichswehr officers to intensively study wartime operations in order to retrain the German army for modern warfare. These studies led to the development of a new doctrine that took existing traditions of *Bewegungskrieg* and updated them with infantry infiltration tactics, tanks, aircraft, gas warfare and motorization. Under Seeckt, the Reichswehr was built for offensive manoeuvre warfare, not the defensive force envisioned by the Allies at Versailles.

Manstein was promoted to *Major* in 1928 and in October 1929 he was assigned to the Truppenamt (troop office), T1 section (operations and planning), which covertly incorporated the functions of the former Generalstab within the guise of an administrative organization. Within the Truppenamt, Manstein was responsible for developing mobilization plans and preparing studies on weapons development. Manstein was at his best in a demanding intellectual environment and he took to these tasks with great relish. In recognition of his contributions, Manstein was promoted to *Oberstleutnant* in April 1931. During his stay in the Truppenamt, Manstein's family continued to grow with the birth of his son Rüdiger.

In the summer of 1931, Oberstleutnant Manstein accompanied the new head of the Truppenamt on a trip to the Soviet Union. Since 1922, Germany had been secretly conducting military training and weapons development in the Soviet Union in order to evade the Versailles Treaty restrictions. Manstein visited the Panzer training unit at Kazan, as well as touring Soviet military facilities in Moscow, Kiev and Kharkov.

In October 1932, Manstein once again had to punch the command ticket in order to further his career and he went to take over II Jäger Bataillon of 4. Preußen-Infanterie-Regiment in Kolberg. Manstein enjoyed his 16 months with the battalion and later referred to this time as one of the best years of his career. Manstein was at Kolberg when Adolf Hitler became Reichskanzler in January 1933 and he began to notice the effect of new policies upon the military enacted by the Nazi regime. Soon, all German military personal – including Manstein – were required to take the new service oath (the *Führereid*) that pledged personal loyalty to Adolf Hitler.

German troops training with the 75mm le IG 18 (light infantry gun). While Manstein was assigned to the Truppenamt in the early 1930s, he was directly involved with infantry training and the integration of new weapons such as the IG 18. (Author's collection)

Wehrmacht service, 1935–39

Hitler moved swiftly to reform the German military and prepare it for rapid expansion to 36 divisions, beginning with the reintroduction of conscription in March 1935. Hitler openly violated the Versailles restrictions by reintroducing the forbidden Generalstab within the Oberkommando des Heeres (OKH). In July, Oberst von Manstein was put in charge of the operations branch of the resurrected Generalstab des Heeres. Generaloberst Werner von Fritsch was the first head of the OKH and General der Artillerie Ludwig Beck was the new chief of the Generalstab. Manstein was directed to write the Wehrmacht's first war plan, for war against France or Czechoslovakia. He wrote *Fall Rot* (*Case Red*) to enable Germany to have a reasonable chance of defending the Ruhr and recommended to Beck that Germany begin a major fortification construction programme along the border with France.

Manstein and Beck were drawn into a doctrinal dispute with the Panzer advocates, led by Generalmajor Oswald Lutz and his outspoken chief of staff, Oberst Heinz Guderian, who were pushing for an independent Panzer arm. Beck had little patience for Guderian and told him that, 'You move too fast for me.' Echoing his chief, Manstein regarded Guderian as a mere 'technician'. As an alternative to Guderian's Panzer divisions, Manstein wrote a memorandum to Beck suggesting the development of *Sturmartellerie* with 75mm howitzers on tank hulls to provide direct fire support to infantry divisions. He proposed equipping each infantry division with a battalion of assault guns by 1940. These units would fall under the control of the artillery branch, which artilleryman Beck regarded as preferable to an independent Panzer branch. Manstein's proposal to create *Sturmartellerie* units did eventually result in the creation of the assault guns that played such a vital

Generalleutnant Manstein as commander of 18. Infanterie-Division in 1938. After his dismissal from the Generalstab following the Blomberg–Fritsch affair, Manstein was sent to troop command and he was uncertain if he had any future career prospects in Hitler's Wehrmacht. (Bundesarchiv, Bild 183-H01757)

role in World War II. However, the offensive-oriented concepts of Lutz and Guderian had won Hitler's approval and the OKH was ordered to form the first three Panzer divisions while the development of assault guns lagged.

Most of the high-ranking Wehrmacht generals, including Beck, Fritsch and Rundstedt, approved of the rearmament programme begun by Hitler and even approved of small wars to eventually 'correct' the borders with Poland and Czechoslovakia, but they were worried about provoking war with a major power before the Wehrmacht was ready. Manstein wrote Operation Plan *Winterübung* (*Winter Exercise*) for the reoccupation of the Rhineland, which resulted in a political triumph for Hitler when the British and French failed to react.

In October 1936, Manstein was promoted to *Generalmajor* and he became Oberquartiermeister I and Beck's deputy. As the second highest man in the Generalstab, Manstein was intimately involved with the rapid expansion and reorganization of the Wehrmacht. In June 1937, Hitler's aggressive intentions became clear when he directed the OKH to prepare plans for a surprise attack on Czechoslovakia. Manstein was one of the key participants who drafted the first version of *Fall Grün* (*Case Green*), as well as *Sonderfall Otto* (*Special Plan Otto*) for the occupation of Austria.

Due to his close personal association with Beck and Fritsch, Manstein was drawn into the growing struggle between the new Nazi leadership and the traditional military leadership for control over the army, which came to a head with the Blomberg–Fritsch scandals of 1938. After both officers were forced to resign, pressure was also put upon Beck to quit due to his growing criticisms of the Nazi regime and he was replaced eventually by General der Artillerie Franz Halder. Amidst this house cleaning, Manstein was removed from the Generalstab and sent to command the 18. Infanterie-Division in Liegnitz. As a close protégé of Beck, Manstein was lucky to remain on active service in the Wehrmacht. Manstein was offended by the abrupt discomfiture of Beck and Fritsch – both of whom he admired – but he avoided any public criticism that might terminate his military career.

Manstein's 18. Infanterie-Division was one of 11 new divisions formed in 1934 and when Manstein took it over from Generalleutnant Hermann Hoth, it was still incomplete. Relieved to be away from the political intrigues in Berlin and promoted to *Generalleutnant*, Manstein later wrote that, 'it was a joy to be standing at the head of this division'. Yet he had little time to prepare his division before the Sudetenland Crisis escalated during the summer of 1938 and Hitler ordered the OKH to prepare to execute *Fall Grün* on 30 September. Manstein's division was assigned to Generaloberst Ritter von Leeb's AOK 2 for a deliberate assault on the formidable Czech border fortifications. However, the British and French politicians folded at the Munich Conference just before X-Day, delivering the Sudetenland to Hitler on a silver platter.

After a brief spell of occupation duty in Czechoslovakia, Manstein was ordered to report to Generaloberst Gerd von Rundstedt's headquarters, located in a monastery at Neisse. Manstein learned that he was appointed chief of staff for Heeresgruppe Süd in *Fall Weiß* (*Case White*), the upcoming invasion of Poland. Manstein was happy to work with Rundstedt – whom he regarded as an old-style, courtly gentleman – and the Ia (operations officer) was Oberst Günther Blumentritt, one of Manstein's few close friends. Together, they worked to implement the deployment plan. This time, there was no diplomatic solution and Heeresgruppe Süd was ordered to invade Poland at 0445hrs on 1 September.

German armour advancing into the Sudetenland in October 1938. Manstein helped develop *Fall Grün* for the attack on Czechoslovakia and then participated in the occupation of the country after the Munich Crisis was resolved. (Bundesarchiv, Bild 146-1970-050-41)

World War II

Poland 1939

As chief of staff of Heeresgruppe Süd, Generalleutnant von Manstein was in a good position to observe the dawn of the new German operational form of war that was soon dubbed blitzkrieg. He was located over 80km (50 miles) behind the front line in his monastery and he communicated with the three subordinate armies by telephone. Furthermore, he was working in an office environment and in his memoirs the only hardship he mentioned was that the sausage they were served in their officers' mess was hard to chew. It is also clear from Manstein's memoirs that he regarded an attack on Poland as justified and he accepted Nazi claims of Polish 'aggression'. Manstein's role was to coordinate the three subordinate armies during the initial stage of the invasion, which rapidly broke through the Polish border defences and raced towards Warsaw.

Two weeks after the end of the Polish campaign, Rundstedt's headquarters was ordered to move west for operations against the Anglo-French. Manstein stopped off at the OKH headquarters in Zossen, south of Berlin and picked up the operations order for *Fall Gelb* (*Case Yellow*) on 21 October. He then proceeded to Koblenz, where Rundstedt's headquarters was now redesignated Heeresgruppe A and put in charge of AOK 12 and 16 assembling near the Belgian border. Blumentritt remained as the Ia but was joined by Oberstleutnant Henning von Tresckow, a clever Generalstab officer of whom Manstein was very fond. The staff was set up in the luxurious Hotel Riesen-Fürstenhof, next to the Rhine.

Sichelschnitt and the French campaign

Hitler was determined to attack the Anglo-French allies as soon as possible after Poland, but no plan for an offensive in the west existed because of his earlier assurances to the Generalstab that the Allies would not fight for Poland. However once Britain and France declared war, the OKH suddenly had to develop a plan in barely a month. Faced with a lack of time and anticipating that Hitler would call off the offensive when he realized how unprepared the Wehrmacht was, Halder simply dusted off the Schlieffen Plan from 1914 and updated it with Panzers and Luftwaffe support. As in 1914, the original *Fall Gelb* plan placed the German *Schwerpunkt* on the right flank in Belgium, but this time Holland would also be invaded. In Halder's plan, Generaloberst Fedor von Bock's Heeresgruppe B, with three armies and six of the ten Panzer divisions, would converge on Brussels and push the Allied forces back towards the Channel coast around Dunkirk. Rundstedt's Heeresgruppe A, with two armies and a single Panzer division, would make a supporting attack through the Ardennes towards Sedan. Halder issued an updated version of the plan on 29 October that allocated all armour to the drive on Brussels.

Once Rundstedt, Manstein and Blumentritt began to examine *Fall Gelb* and the minor role assigned to Heeresgruppe A, they quickly recognized that this plan did not embody the traditional Generalstab concepts of *Bewegungskrieg* and could not lead to decisive *Kesselschlacten* (battles of encirclement). Foremost, Manstein objected to the German main effort being made into Belgium, since he felt that the Allies would expect this move. Under Halder's plan, Manstein expected a massive frontal assault into the teeth of Allied resistance in Belgium, leading to a battle of attrition that Germany could not expect to win.

With Rundstedt's support, Manstein wrote a memo to the OKH that suggested an alternative scheme of manoeuvre that he claimed offered better odds of success than the current plan. Manstein argued that in order to defeat the roughly equivalent Allied armies, the Wehrmacht needed to achieve operational-level surprise by striking the enemy where they least expected it and which offered the chance for the kind of manoeuvre warfare in which the Germans excelled. In order to accomplish this, he argued that the *Schwerpunkt* should be in the centre with Heeresgruppe A and that surprise could be achieved by sending four Panzer divisions through the Ardennes Forest to cross the Meuse River at Sedan. Once a breakthrough was achieved, the Panzer units would

German armour pours through the Ardennes in May 1940, as part of the *Sichelschnitt* plan conceived by Manstein and Guderian. Manstein sought to find a manoeuvre solution to overcome France's defences, rather than the brute-force approach of the original *Fall Gelb*. (HITM Archives)

After crossing the Meuse at Sedan, the German Panzer formations fanned out and cut a swath across northern France to the English Channel. The audacity of Manstein's scheme of manoeuvre caught the Allies flat-footed and rapidly led to decisive success for the Wehrmacht. (HITM Archives)

conduct a *Sichelschnitt* ('sickle-cut') envelopment to reach the Channel coast and thereby trap the main Allied armies in Belgium and following that, a second 'sickle-cut' southwards towards Dijon to cut off the French forces in the Maginot Line. Manstein's concept represented a classic Generalstab solution, by using surprise, concentration and manoeuvre to achieve decisive results. Manstein wrote a total of six memos about his plan to OKH during the winter of 1939–40 but heard nothing in return. Halder, who resented Manstein's efforts to influence OKH planning, ensured that Hitler saw none of these memos. Manstein's concept also benefited from the contributions of Panzer expert General Heinz Guderian, who was also stationed in Koblenz in the autumn of 1939.

Halder was incensed by Manstein's constant barrage of memos and he decided to silence him by having him transferred on 27 January 1940 to take command of the new XXXVIII Armeekorps (AK) forming in Stettin. A third version of *Fall Gelb* was issued on 30 January 1940, which allocated two Panzer divisions to Heeresgruppe A, but which now had a total of three *Schwerpunkts,* spreading the German armour across a broad front. Although Heeresgruppe A was ordered to secure a bridgehead at Sedan, Halder did not envision this occurring until Day 10 of the offensive and Guderian's XIX AK (mot.) was not tasked to conduct any deep penetration on its own.

However, some of Manstein's protégés managed to leak details of his alternate plan to members of Hitler's staff. By this point, Hitler was disenchanted with Halder's plan since it likely would lead to a long struggle of attrition with the Allies, which he wanted to avoid. He became particularly interested in the Sedan area, which seemed to offer a better avenue into north-east France than through Belgium. On 17 February 1940, Manstein and six other senior commanders were ordered to breakfast with the Führer in Berlin and afterwards, Hitler took him aside and asked for his views on *Fall Gelb*. After being briefed by Manstein on his concept, Hitler decided to adopt this new scheme of manoeuvre and ordered the OKH to issue a revised *Fall Gelb*. The new plan increased Heeresgruppe A from 24 to 44 divisions, including the newly formed Panzergruppe Kleist, which would have five Panzer divisions with 1,222 tanks.

Manstein could savour his victory, but only from a distance. When *Fall Gelb* kicked off on 10 May 1940, he was 700km (435 miles) away in Liegnitz and he wrote in his diary, 'it has started and I am sitting at home'. However, his corps was soon ordered to move west by train to join the second-echelon forces, but by the time that he arrived at Rundstedt's new headquarters in Bastogne, the German Panzers had already achieved a clean breakthrough at Sedan and were racing towards the coast. It took some time for Manstein's corps to march from Belgium toward the Somme and it was not until 27 May that his troops arrived near Amiens to take over a 48km (30-mile) stretch of the river line. Manstein's corps was placed under Kluge's AOK 4 and he was assigned to hold the bridgeheads at Abbeville and Amiens. Manstein was chomping at the bit to expand the bridgeheads but Kluge ordered him to remain on the defensive until more German forces reached the Somme.

Once Heeresgruppe A eliminated the trapped Allied forces at Dunkirk, its Panzers turned southwards to finish off France. *Fall Röt* (*Case Red*), the second phase of the German offensive in the west, began with a multi-corps attack across the Somme River on the morning of 5 June. Manstein's XXXVIII AK attacked with two infantry divisions and succeeded in pushing back two French divisions. After two days of fighting, the French were in retreat and Manstein launched a pursuit that succeeded in gaining a crossing over the Seine at Vernon on 9 June and reached the Loire River on 19 June. Although his troops had engaged in only light combat, his corps had advanced 480km (300 miles) by foot in only 17 days.

Manstein's direct participation in the French campaign was short but successful and he was promoted to *General der Infanterie* and awarded the Ritterkreuz der Eisernen Kreuzes. Indirectly, his contribution to revising *Fall Gelb* enabled the Germans to achieve complete surprise and gain the initiative for the entire campaign. Although others, including Hitler, contributed to the final plan, it was Manstein's operational concept that laid the groundwork for the greatest military victory ever achieved by German armies.

OPPOSITE

1. 22–26 June 1941: Manstein's LVI Armeekorps (mot.) advances to Dünaburg, then Pskov and then veers eastwards to encircle Soviet defences around Luga. His corps is them diverted towards Demyansk.
2. Commanding AOK 11, Manstein breaks through the Perekop Peninsula (24 September 1941) before defeating a Soviet counteroffensive along the Sea of Azov. AOK 11 then occupies the bulk of the Crimea (1–14 November) before crushing Soviet resistance at Sevastopol and in the Kerch Peninsula by 4 July 1942.
3. 10 September–1 October 1942: transferred to the Leningrad front, Manstein's AOK 11 defeats the Soviet effort to raise the siege and encircles part of the 2nd Shock Army.
4. As commander of Heeresgruppe Don in November 1942, Manstein conducts Operation *Wintergewitter* to relief the Stalingrad pocket on 12–19 December 1942, but the effort fails.
5. Manstein organizes a defence of the Rostov area with Armeeabteilung Hollidt to enable Heeresgruppe A to escape from the Caucasus, January 1943.
6. Manstein's 'backhand blow' counteroffensive from 20 February to 18 March 1942 inflicts a severe defeat on the Soviet Southwest and Voronezh Fronts, resulting in the recapture of Kharkov.
7. Operation *Zitadelle*, 5–15 July 1943: Manstein's Heeresgruppe Süd fails to reach Kursk.
8. 30 July to 3 August 1942: Manstein commits two Panzer corps to crush the Soviet breakthrough across the Mius River.
9. After Vatutin's offensive ruptures his left flank on 3 August, Kharkov is lost on 22 August and the 4. Panzerarmee is pushed westwards.
10. Vatutin captures Kiev on 6 November. Manstein mounts a major counteroffensive at Zhitomir on 15–25 November and Radomyshl on 6–23 December, but fails to recapture Kiev or encircle the Soviet tank armies.
11. 24–28 January 1944: Operation *Watutin*, Manstein counterattacks the 1st Tank Army, inflicting significant losses.
12. 1–17 February 1944: Operation *Wanda*, Manstein commits two Panzerkorps to rescue the 56,000 German troops trapped in the Korsun Pocket, which succeeds in rescuing two-thirds of the encircled forces.
13. 28–30 March 1944: when a new Soviet offensive encircles most of Hube's 1. Panzerarmee, Manstein begins organizing a rescue effort but is relieved of command before it occurs.

Manstein's campaigns in the east, 1941–44

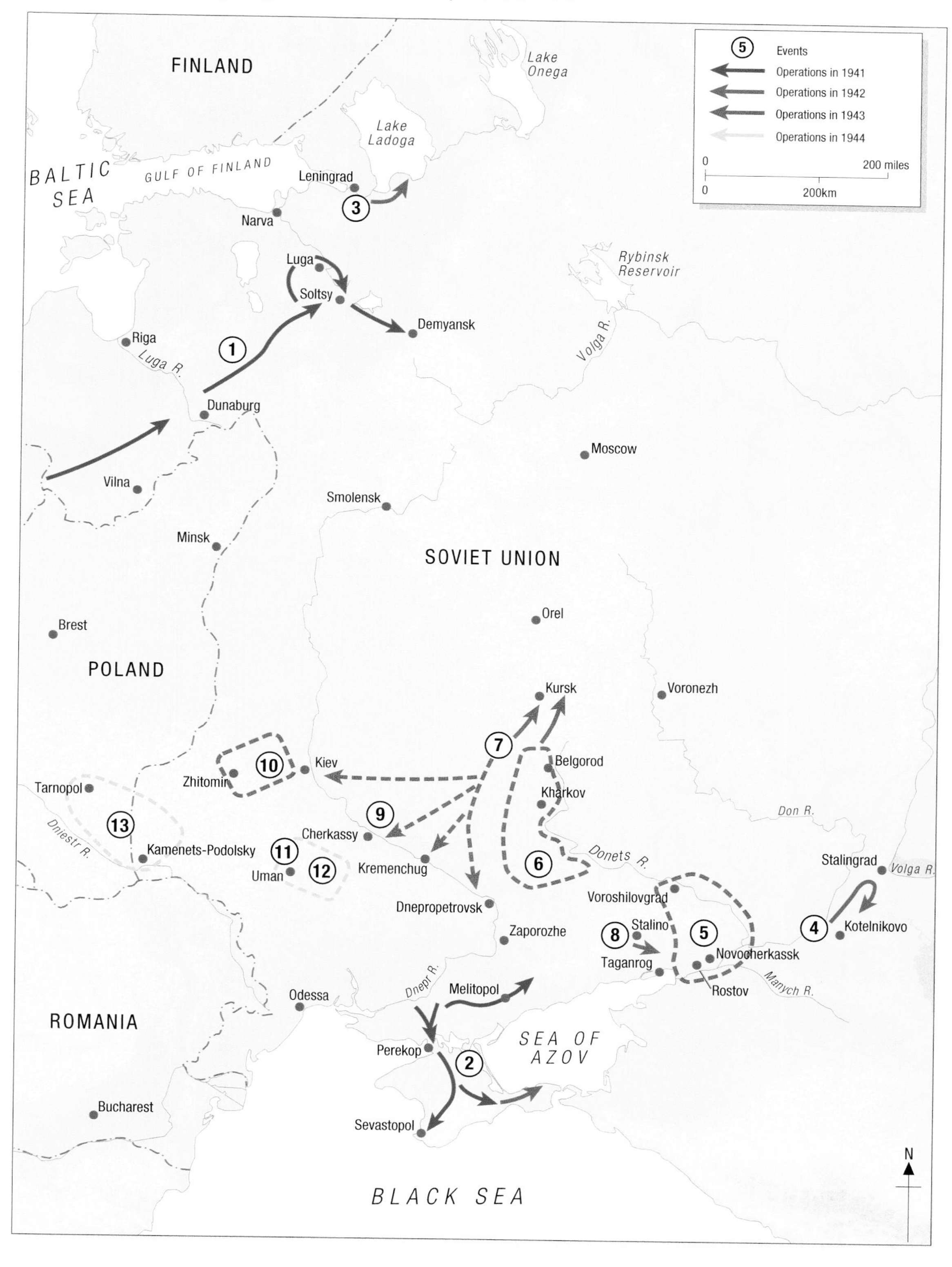

Seelöwe and *Barbarossa*

After the French armistice, XXXVIII AK was moved to the Boulogne area to prepare for a possible invasion of England. Under Operation *Seelöwe* (*Sealion*) – the invasion plan developed by the OKH and the Kriegsmarine – 380 barges would carry Manstein's corps from Boulogne to Beach 'D' off Bexhill. However, the Luftwaffe failed to achieve air superiority over the Channel and Hitler decided to postpone the operation. In his memoirs, Manstein regarded the invasion as risky but said that it was the only strategy that offered potentially decisive results against Great Britain. With *Seelöwe* postponed, Manstein passed much of the autumn of 1940 either in Paris or home on leave, as did many of his troops. The war seemed as good as won.

When Hitler ordered the OKH to begin developing a plan to invade the Soviet Union, Halder ensured that Manstein was not involved. Instead, in February 1941 Manstein was ordered to take command of the LVI AK (mot.) headquarters, forming in the quiet spa town of Bad Salzuflen. On 30 March, Manstein was one of 250 senior German officers briefed on Operation *Barbarossa*. He learned that his unit would be one of two motorized corps assigned to Generaloberst Erich Höpner's 4. Panzergruppe in Generalfeldmarschall Ritter von Leeb's Heeresgruppe Nord. The other motorized formation was the XLI AK (mot.) under General der Panzertruppe Hans George Reinhardt. The objective was to overrun the Soviet forces in the Baltic States and then drive rapidly on Leningrad, which was expected to fall within six to eight weeks. Two weeks prior to the invasion, Manstein and other senior commanders were briefed on the Führer's intent to fight a campaign of extermination in the Soviet Union, including the notorious *Kommissar Befehl* (commissar order) that required the summary execution of all captured Soviet political officers.

Manstein was assigned the 8. Panzer-Division, 3. Infanterie-Division (mot.) and 290. Infanterie-Division, meaning that his corps was only partly motorized. His corps moved into its assembly area in the woods near Tilsit in late May 1941 and Manstein arrived only six days before the start of *Barbarossa*. Höpner tasked both Manstein and Reinhardt to punch through the relatively thinly held Soviet border defences, encircle any units of the Soviet 8th Army that got in their way and advance rapidly to seize separate crossings over the Dvina River.

Manstein as corps commander, conferring with General der Panzertruppe Erich Brandenberger, commander of the 8. Panzer-Division, in the summer of 1941. Brandenberger's division was roughly handled at the battle of Soltsy. (Bundesarchiv, Bild 101I-209-0086-12, Fotograf: Koch)

Drive on Leningrad

Manstein attacked across the Nieman River at 0300hrs on 22 June 1941 with his 8. Panzer-Division and 290. Infanterie-Division. The attack struck the lightly defended boundary between the Soviet 8th and 11th Armies, and 8. Panzer-Division advanced 70km (44 miles) on the first day. Unknown to Manstein, part of the Soviet 3rd Mechanized Corps made an attack into the flank of 4. Panzergruppe but passed right by Manstein's spearheads and engaged in a major tank battle with Reinhardt's corps around Raseiniai.

While Reinhardt was busy fending off the Soviet armour, Manstein's corps continued its rapid advance to the Dvina River along the Dvinsk highway against negligible opposition. On the morning of 26 June, after an advance of 315km (196 miles) in 100 hours, the lead *Kampfgruppe* of 8. Panzer-Division and a company of Brandenburg troops in Soviet uniforms seized both the road and railway bridges over the Dvina at Daugavpils intact. Manstein's dash across Lithuania had accomplished the *Panzergruppe*'s intermediate objective at the cost of only 365 casualties. However, the German bridgehead was precarious, since Manstein was 100km (62 miles) ahead of the rest of Heeresgruppe Nord and it took another two days for his infantry to reach the bridgehead. Even worse, the rapid advance had consumed 5.5 VS (*Verbrauchssatz*) of fuel – equivalent to 545 tons of gasoline – that left his spearhead virtually immobilized. Lacking prior direct experience with armoured force logistics, Manstein simply ran his corps forwards at maximum speed until it ran out of fuel and had no hope of immediate resupply. Nor had Manstein's dash done very much damage to the Soviet 8th or 11th Armies, since his corps took fewer than 5,000 prisoners in the first two weeks of the offensive and no major units were overrun or encircled.

The Soviets were determined to recapture the bridges over the Dvina and subjected Manstein's corps to persistent attacks from tactical bombers. On the morning of 28 June, the Soviet 21st Mechanized Corps under General-Major Dmitri Lelyushenko attacked Manstein's bridgehead with 60 BT-7 light tanks and several battalions of motorized infantry. Lelyushenko was a very experienced and combat-savvy commander; for the first time, Manstein was up against a capable opponent. The Soviet counterattack pressed Manstein's isolated, out-of-fuel corps fairly hard but Lelyushenko's corps was in even worse shape and after losing most of his tanks he had to break off the attack and retire northwards.

Once the rest of Heeresgruppe Nord reached the Dvina River, Manstein's corps was refueled and he was given the SS-Division 'Totenkopf' for the pursuit of Lelyushenko's forces. However, Manstein's pursuit was sluggish and it was Reinhardt who made greater progress towards Leningrad, capturing Pskov

Left:
An abandoned Soviet KV-2 heavy tank in Lithuania, June 1941. These tanks proved to be a severe shock to the *Panzertruppen*. Manstein's rapid dash to Dünaburg meant that he missed a head-on clash with these giants and left Reinhardt's corps to fight the Soviet armour on its own. (Bundesarchiv, Bild 101I-209-0091-11, Fotograf: Nägele)

Right:
German armour advancing through a forest track towards Leningrad. Manstein's corps was caught strung out along these type of roads by the Soviet counterattack at Soltsy on 15 July 1941. (Bundesarchiv, Bild 101I-209-0074-16A, Fotograf: Zoll)

A PzKpfw IV medium tank of the 8. Panzer-Division bypasses a destroyed bridge, July 1941. German armour usually breached river lines before the Soviets could form effective defences. (Bundesarchiv, Bild 101I-209-0052-35A, Fotograf: Koch)

on 8 July. With the capture of Pskov, Höpner hoped to get his Panzers across the Luga River before the Soviets could establish a new defensive line, so he decided to conduct a classic pincer attack on the Soviet concentration around Luga by sending Reinhardt's corps westwards to cross the river, while Manstein's corps would move to the north-east towards Novgorod. Manstein's corps marched towards Lake Il'men, with the 8. Panzer-Division in the lead. Manstein's troops were able to advance fairly rapidly and had only sporadic contact for the first several days.

Although the Soviets were frantically trying to establish a strong defensive position behind the Luga River, Marshal Kliment E. Voroshilov decided to use his limited reserves to conduct a spoiling attack. Noticing that the two German motorized corps were too far apart to provide mutual support, he ordered the 11th Army to counterattack Manstein's corps near Soltsy. Voroshilov sent his chief of staff, Nikolai Vatutin, to organize the counterattack.

On the morning of 15 July, the 8. Panzer-Division was strung out along the main road east of Soltsy, with virtually no flank protection. Manstein's corps command post was west of Soltsy and the 3. Infanterie-Division (mot.) was even further back. Unknown to Manstein, General-Major Ivan Lazarev had assembled two full-strength units – the 21st Tank Division and the 70th Rifle Division – in the woods north of Soltsy, while three weak rifle divisions from the 22nd Rifle Corps were massing south of Soltsy. Vatutin ordered these two groups to mount a coordinated pincer attack to cut the main road behind the Germans. Thus, it was a great surprise when the 8. Panzer-Division was attacked in force on its left flank by waves of enemy infantry, supported by over 100 T-26 light tanks, considerable artillery and even some air support. As the 8. Panzer-Division recoiled back towards Soltsy, the southern assault group severed the road behind Soltsy and soon the 8. Panzer-Division was encircled. In desperation, Manstein ordered the 8. Panzer-Division to fight its way out of the encirclement and arranged for limited air resupply. After two days of heavy fighting, the 8. Panzer-Division finally broke out of the encirclement but was so battered that it had to be pulled back into reserve to refit, leaving Manstein with no armour. Eventually, Höpner sent reinforcements and the exhausted Soviet assault groups called off the counteroffensive. Due to Vatutin's counteroffensive, Manstein was unable to fulfil his mission to get behind the Luga line and the battle of Soltsy was his first defeat.

After Soltsy, Manstein's command was reduced to only a single division for two weeks, but in early August he was given two more infantry divisions to conduct frontal attacks against the main Soviet defences around Luga while Reinhardt's Panzers executed a single envelopment from their bridgehead. Soviet resistance was fierce, but Manstein was on the verge of linking up with

The battle of Soltsy, 15–17 July 1941

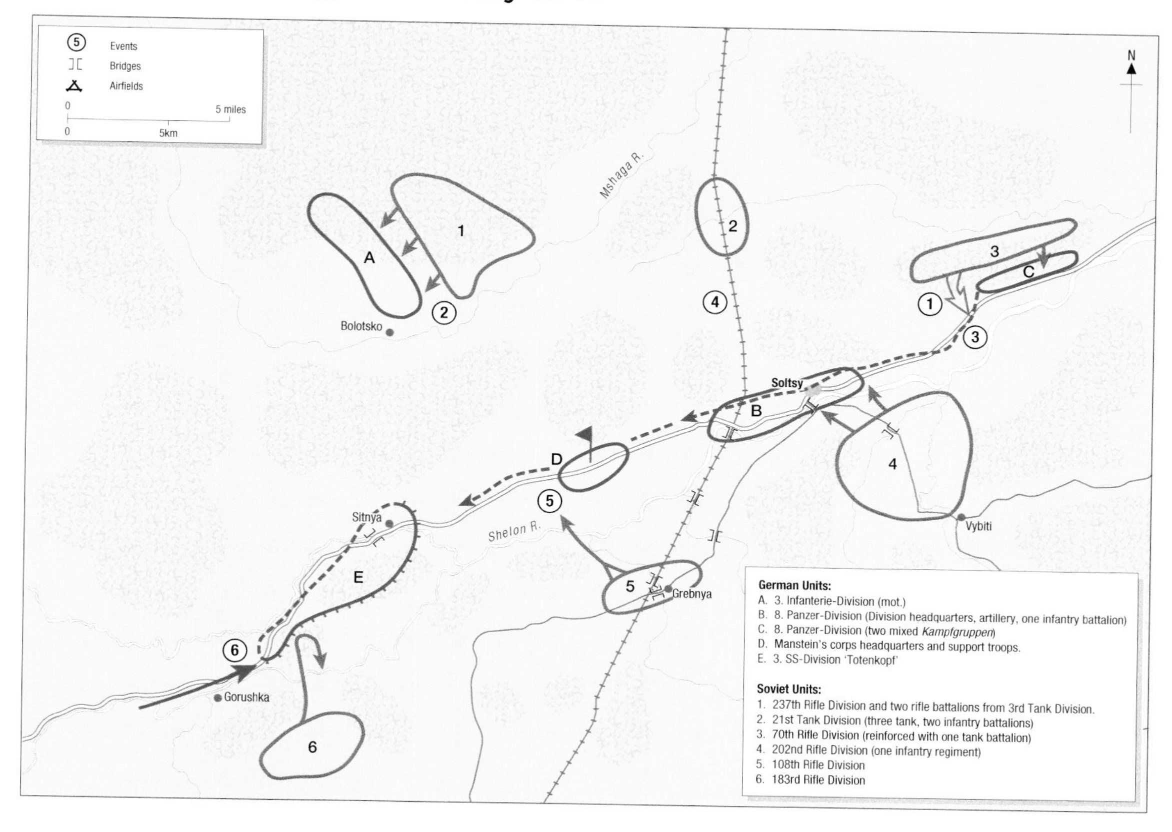

1. 15 July, morning: the 70th Rifle Division attacks and seizes the road behind the spearhead of the 8. Panzer-Division.
2. The 237th Rifle Division launches multiple attacks on the German 3. Infanterie-Division (mot), preventing it from going to help the 8. Panzer-Division.
3. 15–16 July: the spearhead of the 8. Panzer-Division manages to fight its way out of the encirclement and retreats westward to Soltsy.
4. 16 July: the Soviet 21st Tank attacks and threatens to cut the road west of Soltsy, while the weak 202nd Rifle Division attacks Soltsy from the south. Surrounded on three sides, the 8. Panzer-Division abandons Soltsy.
5. 17 July: as the Soviet XXII Rifle Corps attacks with the 180th and 183rd Rifle Divisions to cut the main road to Soltsy, the 8. Panzer-Division continues to retreat westwards.
6. 18 July: The 3. SS-Division 'Totenkopf' arrives and clears the road to enable the battered 8. Panzer-Division to move into reserve. Manstein re-establishes a new corps front line around Sitnya.

Reinhardt's Panzers when once again, Marshal Voroshilov decided to disrupt German operations with a counterstroke of his own.

On 12 August, the Soviet 11th and 34th Armies attacked with ten divisions against the three divisions of the German X AK in Staraya Russa. This was virtually a repeat of the Soltsy counterattack – except on a larger scale – and within three days the Soviets had isolated X AK, presenting Heeresgruppe Nord with a serious crisis. Since Reinhardt's Panzers were too far away to help, Leeb decided to use Manstein's corps to mount a relief operation. Manstein was given the SS-Division 'Totenkopf' and the 3. Infanterie-Division (mot.) to mount a two-division pincer attack against General-Major Kuzma M. Kachanov's 34th Army on 19 August. Luftwaffe close air support helped Manstein's attack make rapid progress and he

Left:
Russian prisoners taken by Heeresgruppe Nord, July 1941. Manstein's corps took few prisoners during the advance on Leningrad; his troops did comply with Hitler's *Komissar Befehl*. Throughout his career in Russia, Manstein turned a blind eye to the fate of enemy prisoners. (Bundesarchiv, Bild 101I-010-0919-39, Fotograf: Georg Schmidt)

Right:
German troops executing Soviet 'partisans' in the Heeresgruppe Nord area of operations near Leningrad in September 1941. (Bundesarchiv, Bild 101I-212-0221-06, Fotograf: Thiede)

not only re-established ground communications with X AK but encircled elements of five Soviet divisions. Manstein claimed that his corps captured 12,000 prisoners within the *Kessel* and there is no doubt that he inflicted a heavy defeat upon Kachanov, who was executed for his failure.

Despite success at Staraya Russa, Leeb decided to detach Manstein's corps to support AOK 16's drive eastwards towards Demyansk, due to increasing Soviet activity in this sector. Near Demyansk on 12 September, Manstein was informed that he was being given command of AOK 11 in Heeresgruppe Süd and he departed the next day.

As a corps commander, Manstein demonstrated that he was an aggressive leader who understood how to conduct *Bewegungskrieg* in order to achieve operational-level success. However, he accomplished fewer of his missions that his peer Reinhardt and his corps only had a Panzer division attached about half the time. During much of the 12-week drive on Leningrad, he was actually leading just infantry formations. Manstein's operations in Lithuania and Latvia did reveal that he still had a great deal to learn about mechanized force logistics and properly identifying restricted terrain. More worrisome, the surprise at Soltsy indicates that Manstein did not anticipate enemy actions, which is a mistake that he would repeat in the future.

Conquest of the Crimea 1941–42

Manstein arrived at AOK 11 headquarters in Nikolyaev on 17 September, right after that formation had gotten across the Dnepr River at Berislav. At this point, AOK 11 consisted of XLIX Gebirgs-Armeekorps, XXX AK and LIV AK, with a total of nine German divisions, and the attached 3rd Romanian Army. Generalfeldmarschall Gerd von Rundstedt, commander of Heeresgruppe Süd, assigned AOK 11 two missions after crossing the Dnepr: pursue the retreating Soviet forces eastwards to Rostov and conquer the Crimea.

Initially, Manstein tried to accomplish both missions, even though this pulled his army in different directions. He sent General der Kavallerie Erik Hansen's LIV AK with three divisions to open an entrance to the Crimea by capturing the Perekop Isthmus, while the rest of his army advanced towards Melitopol. Hansen spent six days battering his way through the 8km-wide (5-mile) neck of the Perekop Isthmus, until the 51st Army began to retreat in disarray. However, Manstein's hopes for exploiting this success were dashed when a Soviet counteroffensive near Melitopol overran a Romanian brigade. Manstein was forced to commit the SS-Division (mot.) 'Leibstandarte SS Adolf Hitler' to save the situation in the east, which left him no fresh units to exploit the success gained at Perekop. Instead, he launched fixing attacks against the front of the Soviet 9th and 18th Armies, while Kleist's 1. Panzergruppe enveloped the hapless Red Army divisions from the north, trapping them against the Sea of Azov by 7 October.

Manstein's attempts to seize Sevastopol in November–December 1941 failed and he was forced to mount a winter siege of the city. (HITM Archives)

After the battle of the Sea of Azov, Rundstedt reduced Manstein's AOK 11 to six German infantry divisions and the Romanians, but allowed him to focus just on the Crimea. Hansen's corps was badly outnumbered by the Soviet 51st Army, which occupied fortified positions near Ishun at the southern end of the Perekop Isthmus. A huge set-piece battle began on 18 October and continued for ten days as the Germans slowly fought their way through the Soviet defences. When the Soviet troops began to fall back into the interior of the Crimea, Manstein began a vigorous pursuit with extemporized motorized columns, Romanian cavalry and force-marching infantry that kept the enemy on the run. German troops entered Simferopol on 1 November – where Manstein set up his new headquarters – and Kerch was overrun on 16 November. The Soviet Navy established hasty landward defences around the fortress of Sevastopol, but Manstein hoped to take it before reinforcements arrived by sea. He tried a probing attack on 10 November that failed due to lack of heavy artillery and air support. Resigned to a siege, Manstein ordered XXX and LIV AK to invest the city, while the newly assigned XLII AK and the Romanians guarded the eastern coast of the Crimea.

By the beginning of December 1941, Manstein's AOK 11 in the Crimea was the only Wehrmacht formation still attacking on the Eastern Front. Yet Manstein's supply situation was poor and he had little artillery or air support to mount a deliberate attack on a fortified area. Nevertheless, he launched a six-division offensive against Sevastopol on 17 December that gained some ground but failed to capture the city. After AOK 11 suffered 8,500 casualties, Manstein called off the offensive and settled into a siege. However, on 26 December the Soviet 51st Army landed 5,000 troops at Kerch and three days later the 44th Army landed at Feodosiya. Manstein had underestimated the threat of Soviet amphibious operations and he left only one division from Generalleutnant Hans Graf von Sponeck's XLII AK to guard over 150km (93 miles) of coastline. Sponeck succeeded in smashing the smaller Kerch landing but the loss of Feodosiya threatened to cut off his troops so he asked Manstein permission to withdraw. Manstein refused the request. Sponeck decided to retreat without orders and conducted a

100km (62-mile) forced march that saved his troops from encirclement, then formed a new front west of Feodosiya that contained the Soviet landings. In spite of the fact that disaster had been averted, Manstein relieved Sponeck of command and reported his disobedience to the OKH. Even though he was a recipient of the Ritterkreuz, Sponeck was hauled before a court of honour in Germany and sentenced to death, but Hitler commuted the sentence to six years in the military prison at Germersheim.

Manstein sent XXX AK to reinforce the hard-pressed XLII AK and then launched an amazing winter counterattack on 15 January 1942 that succeeded in recapturing Feodosiya and inflicting over 16,000 Soviet casualties. However, AOK 11 had exhausted its last reserves in retaking Feodosiya and the Stavka used the subsequent lull to reinforce the newly formed Crimean Front under General-Lieutenant Dmitri T. Kozlov.

During the period of February–April 1942, Manstein found himself conducting a two-front defensive campaign with greatly inferior resources. The Soviet Black Sea Fleet poured reinforcements and supplies into Sevastopol – mocking German claims that the city was under siege – and General-Major Ivan Petrov's Coastal Army was rebuilt into a powerful force that actually outnumbered Hansen's besieging force. Stalin was quick to note that together, the forces of Petrov and Kozlov outnumbered Manstein's AOK 11 by two to one and he bullied both commanders into launching premature offensives. Between February and May 1942, Manstein repulsed three Soviet offensives, which failed to break the AOK 11 siege lines. However, when Heeresgruppe Süd sent the 22. Panzer-Division to reinforce the Crimea, Manstein used it in a poorly planned counterattack against prepared Soviet defences that failed with the loss of 32 tanks. This counterattack was a sobering lesson for Manstein in the use of Panzers; trying to breach enemy minefields and anti-tank ditches without support from pioneers, infantry and artillery was suicidal. Like many German commanders, Manstein had been conditioned by the easy victories of 1940–41 to think that Panzer divisions could overcome all opposition on their own, but now he learned that proper combined arms tactics were required to overcome a dug-in and determined opponent.

Soviet naval infantry landing near Kerch on 26 December 1941, threatening to annihilate Manstein's thin covering forces. Manstein had not expected amphibious landings during the winter and underestimated Soviet resourcefulness. (RIA Novosti, 90324)

After Kozlov's attacks petered out in April, Manstein flew to meet with Hitler at the Wolfsschanze in East Prussia to receive guidance for the 1942 campaign. Hitler listened to Manstein's operational plans for dealing with both Soviet positions and for once, gave his commander on the spot a relatively free hand. Manstein informed Hitler that he intended to crush the Soviet Crimean Front with a surprise offensive in May known as Operation *Trappenjagd* (*Bustard Hunt*), then once the Kerch Peninsula was cleared, to concentrate all of AOK 11 for a mighty assault upon Sevastopol in July known as Operation *Störfang* (Sturgeon Haul).

Manstein succeeded in concentrating five infantry, one Panzer and two Romanian divisions against Kozlov's front, which had been reinforced to three armies with the equivalent of 20 divisions. Kozlov constructed three lines of defence across the Parpach narrows, with his 44th and 51st Armies up front and the 47th Army in reserve. Given that Manstein's forces were outnumbered two to one and that swamps protected the southern portion of the Soviet front, Kozlov thought that his position was impregnable. Instead, Manstein launched one of the most amazing attacks of World War II on the morning of 8 May 1942. As in the *Sichelschnitt* plan, Manstein placed his *Schwerpunkt* in the worst terrain, attacking through the swamps to pulverize the two front-line divisions of the 44th Army with massed artillery and Stuka dive-bombing. Meanwhile, Manstein employed his secret weapon – the 902. Sturmboote Kommando – to land a reinforced infantry company behind the main Soviet defences. In just 3½ hours, the Soviet front was pierced and Manstein pushed his second echelon forces through to widen the breach. Richthofen's Fliegerkorps VIII – whose arrival Soviet intelligence had not detected – launched a series of devastating attacks that quickly gained air superiority over the Crimea. Before Kozlov was even aware of the extent of the danger posed by the German breakthrough, Manstein committed the 22. Panzer-Division on the second day of the offensive, and this time it committed a perfect enveloping attack that pinned the bulk of the 51st Army against the Sea of Azov. After that, Manstein quickly force-marched infantry and small motorized units to overrun the eastern Kerch Peninsula, while the rest of his army finished off the trapped Soviet troops. With his command shattered and its survivors retreating in disorder toward the port of Kerch, Kozlov ordered an evacuation to the Taman Peninsula, but was only able to save 37,000 of his 212,000 troops before Kerch was captured on 15 May. Manstein had demolished three Soviet armies in just one week and at the cost of only 3,397 casualties. Now, he could turn to deal unhindered with Sevastopol.

After the fall of Kerch, the Stavka rushed 5,000 reinforcements to Petrov's army in Sevastopol, but the Soviets did not anticipate the scale and intensity of Operation *Störfang* when it began on 2 June. Manstein assembled over 900 medium and heavy guns, which he used to soften up the defences with a five-day bombardment while Fliegerkorps VIII pounded the harbour areas. After methodically eliminating a number of the forward Soviet positions, Manstein once again used Hansen's LIV AK as a battering ram, gouging a

German *Feldgendarmerie* round up civilians in Simferopol in January 1942. Despite the fact that his headquarters was located in this city, Manstein later claimed that he was unaware that over 14,000 civilians were executed here. This photo clearly shows that Manstein's own AOK 11 soldiers were involved in roundups, in accordance with his directive of 20 November 1941. (Bundesarchiv, Bild 183-B18164, Fotograf: Hans Zündorf)

Manstein as commander of AOK 11 in early 1942, wearing his Ritterkreuz and recently awarded Romanian Order of Michael the Brave, 3rd Class. (Bundesarchiv, Bild 101I-231-0718-12A)

deep dent in the northern Soviet lines on 7 June. The XXX AK, under General der Artillerie Maximilian Fretter-Pico, was assigned to conduct a supporting attack against the southern Soviet defences, but Manstein was dissatisfied with Fretter-Pico's sluggish and unimaginative attacks. The Romanian Mountain Corps was also attached to AOK 11 for *Störfang,* but Manstein used them to hold the relatively quiet central sector. Early on, it became obvious that Operation *Störfang* would be a battle of attrition, consuming ammunition and infantry at a prodigious rate and victory would go to the side that maintained its combat effectiveness the longest. Since he was attacking the equivalent of eight heavily fortified enemy divisions with only nine of his own divisions, Manstein ensured that he had as many combat multipliers as possible to increase the effectiveness of his assaults. He assigned two pioneer battalions to each assault division to breach obstacles and he managed to get three assault gun battalions for close support.

Manstein observed the initial ground assaults from a concealed observation post, but he did not visit the front lines much during the offensive, due to the threat from persistent sniper and mortar fire. Unlike commanders such as Erwin Rommel or Heinz Guderian, Manstein was not comfortable with front-line leadership and preferred to operate from a fixed command post where he could best coordinate his three corps commanders, his artillery and Richthofen's air support. His relationship with the Romanian corps commander, General-Major Gheorge Avramescu, deteriorated during the campaign when Manstein made it clear that he didn't trust the Romanian troops. Yet when the Romanian mountain infantry were committed to action in the final stages of the battle, they performed well despite Manstein's misgivings.

By late June, Manstein's AOK 11 had made considerable progress in reducing Sevastopol, but his infantry units were badly depleted, much of the heavy artillery was running out of ammunition and Fliegerkorps VIII was due to transfer north to support Operation *Blau*. Manstein decided to gamble before his offensive ran out of steam; he brought in the 902. Sturmboote Kommando to enable Hansen's LIV AK to make a surprise night crossing of Severnaya Bay, while Fretter-Pico's XXX AK made a night assault on the Sapun Ridge on 29 June. Both attacks achieved success, which fatally compromised the Soviet defence. When they realized that their defence was crumbling, the Soviets began a last-second evacuation that saved Petrov and the senior leadership, but left the bulk of the Coastal Army in the lurch. German troops entered the ruins of Sevastopol on 1 July and all resistance was crushed within three days. Manstein had captured one of

the strongest fortresses on earth at the cost of over 35,000 German and Romanian casualties. The Soviets lost 113,000 troops killed or captured, with seven divisions annihilated. It was a stunning if costly victory and Hitler was satisfied enough to award Manstein his *Generalfeldmarschall*'s baton on 1 July. Manstein had reached the pinnacle of his military career.

Above:
Manstein's secret weapon in the Crimea – a *Sturmboote* carrying a squad of infantry. Twice he succeeded in unhinging strong Soviet defences by infiltrating infantry across unprotected water flanks and he intended to use them again at Leningrad to cross the Neva River. (Bundesarchiv, Bild 101I-266-0058-14, Fotograf: Vorpahl)

Manstein had fought a nine-month campaign in the Crimea that was virtually independent from the rest of the Wehrmacht effort in the Soviet Union, receiving only sporadic support from Heeresgruppe Süd. During this period, he smashed four Soviet armies and inflicted in excess of 360,000 casualties upon the enemy. The restrictive terrain in the Crimea forced Manstein to fight the kind of campaign that offered few opportunities for *Bewegungskrieg*, but he seized these opportunities when they did arise and he fought a far more intelligent battle of position than Paulus would fight at Stalingrad in the autumn of 1942. However, Manstein's triumph was tarnished by the disloyalty that he demonstrated to his subordinates and Romanian allies, as well as his acquiescence to the SS execution of thousands of Soviet prisoners and civilians after the fall of Sevastopol.

Return to the Leningrad front, August–November 1942

After the fall of Sevastopol, Manstein spent several weeks in Romania on vacation and when he returned, new orders from the OKH directed AOK 11 to proceed by rail to join Generalfeldmarschall Georg von Küchler's Heeresgruppe Nord in the siege lines outside Leningrad. In Hitler's mind, Manstein had proven himself an expert in siege warfare and was the logical choice to bring the year-long siege of Leningrad to a successful conclusion.

When Manstein reached the Leningrad front on 27 August 1942, the period of mobile operations was long gone and this area had settled into positional warfare reminiscent of World War I. Due to transportation difficulties, AOK 11 would not arrive all at once, but trickled northwards over a two-month period.

Manstein was dubious about taking Leningrad, since his experience at Sevastopol taught him that a battle of attrition in an urban area defended by 200,000 enemy troops would probably bleed his forces white. Furthermore, Heeresgruppe Nord lacked sufficient pioneers, artillery, assault guns, air support and even ammunition to use the kind of tactics that had worked at Sevastopol. Not wanting a Pyrrhic victory, Manstein developed plan *Nordlicht* (*Northern Lights*) that employed a typically bold scheme of manoeuvre. He intended to use five infantry divisions and his available artillery to achieve a penetration of the Soviet fortified lines south of Leningrad and then conduct a night assault crossing of the Neva River. Once a bridgehead was secured, Manstein would push the 12. Panzer-Division and four fresh infantry divisions across the river to outflank the Soviet 55th Army and then push north to sever

Opposite:
Soviet prisoners captured by the 22. Panzer-Division during Operation *Trappenjagd* in the Crimea, May 1942. Manstein's troops captured 147,000 prisoners during the operation – the largest haul he ever took. (Bundesarchiv, B 145 Bild-F016237-0022A)

A destroyed 305mm gun turret at Fort Maxim Gorky in Sevastopol, June 1942. Manstein reduced this fortress by careful use of combined-arms tactics, aided by overwhelming Luftwaffe close air support. (Bundesarchiv, N 1603 Bild-117, Fotograf: Horst Grund)

the Leningrad–Osinovets railway line. If he could cut Leningrad's tenuous supply lines across Lake Ladoga, the city could be quickly starved into submission and he would thereby avoid a costly city fight as in Stalingrad.

Meanwhile, Soviet intelligence detected the arrival of AOK 11 elements near Leningrad and concluded that a German offensive was imminent. The Stavka ordered General Kirill Meretskov's Volkhov Front and General-Lieutenant Leonid Govorov's Leningrad Front to conduct a pincer attack upon the Siniavino Heights in order to disrupt the German preparations for an offensive. On 27 August – the day that Manstein arrived – both Soviet fronts attacked. Govorov's initial efforts to get across the Neva River failed, leaving Meretskov to attack the Siniavino Heights with his 8th Army. Using their large superiority in numbers, the Soviet infantry succeeded in pushing a deep bulge into the German lines, into which Meretskov then pushed part of the 2nd Shock Army.

Schwerpunkt! German troops cross the Soviet anti-tank ditch near Parpach during Operation *Trappenjagd*, 8 May 1942

Manstein began Operation *Trappenjagd* on the morning of 8 May 1942 with the objective of destroying the three Soviet armies in the Kerch Peninsula. Although his forces were outnumbered, Manstein decided to surprise his opponents by making his main effort – his *Schwerpunkt* – in the swampy terrain south of Parpach. The Soviets did not expect an attack in this sector, but dug an 11m-wide (36ft) anti-tank ditch just to be sure. However, Manstein ordered XXX AK to breach the anti-tank ditch and create a penetration corridor for the 22. Panzer-Division to exploit. The 28. leichte-Division was the tip of Manstein's spear and he ensured that it was reinforced with a battalion of assault guns, assault pioneers, massed Stuka sorties and the corps artillery. Armed with this support, the *Jäger* blasted their way through the outer Soviet defences and reached the ditch before dawn. Here, the *Jäger* have just secured the far side of the obstacle, while assault guns, artillery and Stukas keep the enemy's heads down. Due to Manstein's concentration of overwhelming force at the decisive point, he was able to breach a seemingly impregnable Soviet defence using fire and manoeuvre. Once this penetration was made and German armour began to cross the anti-tank ditch into the Soviet rear areas, the defence of the entire Soviet Crimean Front was rapidly compromised, leading to the greatest victory in Manstein's career.

Manstein and his staff aboard his command train on the Leningrad front, September 1942. Oberst Theodor Busse (Ia) is on his right and Generalmajor Karl Friedrich Schulz (chief of staff) is on his left. (Author's collection)

An offensive originally intended only as a spoiling attack suddenly appeared capable of reopening a land corridor to Leningrad.

Hitler realized that the entire siege of Leningrad was in jeopardy and he ordered Manstein to take personal command of all the forces around the Siniavino Heights and to use some of the assault divisions preparing for the attack on Leningrad to eliminate the Soviet salient. Although Manstein had to feed two of his veteran divisions into battle piecemeal to block any further Soviet advance, he realized that the best long-term solution was to conduct a pincer attack to cut off the Soviet salient. Manstein attacked on 21 September with six divisions and succeeded in encircling the salient and trapping parts of the 8th Army and the 2nd Shock Army. Manstein then spent the next three weeks reducing the *Kessel* with artillery and air bombardments. By mid-October, Manstein's AOK 11 had eliminated the *Kessel* and taken 12,000 prisoners, but it suffered over 10,000 casualties itself. Heeresgruppe Nord decided to postpone *Nordlicht* until its units could be refitted.

While mulling over the prospects for mounting *Nordlicht* in spring 1943, Manstein received news on 30 October that his eldest son, Leutnant Gero von Manstein, had been killed the previous day near Lake Il'men by Soviet air attack. Manstein had dined with Gero on 18 October and his death took the gloss off victory in the first battle of Lake Ladoga.

The Stalingrad relief operation, December 1942

While Manstein stabilized the German front around Leningrad, the Wehrmacht was involved in a death struggle with the Red Army at Stalingrad. General der Panzertruppe Friedrich Paulus' AOK 6 and part of Generaloberst Herman Hoth's 4. Panzerarmee had reached the Volga River in early September 1942, but after two months of intense combat the Soviets still held part of Stalingrad. A crisis developed when the Soviet Southwest Front under General Nikolai Vatutin and the Stalingrad Front under General-Colonel Andrei Yeremenko attacked the Romanian 3rd and 4th Armies guarding Paulus' flanks on 19 November and achieved spectacular breakthroughs. With the Romanians disintegrating, Hitler and the OKH realized that AOK 6 was in danger of being encircled and decided to establish Heeresgruppe Don to deal with the crisis. Having just crushed the Soviet offensive at Leningrad, Hitler felt that Manstein was the right man for the job and picked him to lead the new formation on 20 November.

Manstein decided to take his chief of staff, Generalmajor Karl Friedrich Schulz and his Ia, Oberst Theodor Busse, with him on this new assignment. However, Manstein did not appear to be in a great hurry to reach his new command and took nearly a week to reach the area of operations, during which events were moving very rapidly. In his memoirs, he claimed that 'the weather was too bad for flying' and this required him to go by train the entire way, but in his memoirs, Friedrich W. von Mellenthin reports that he travelled by air from Rastenberg to Rostov in a single day in order to reach Heeresgruppe Don.

By the time that Manstein arrived at Novocherkassk near Rostov on 26 November, Vatutin's and Yeremenko's forces had already linked up at Kalach, surrounding over 250,000 German and Romanian troops in the Stalingrad Pocket. General der Infanterie Karl Hollidt quickly formed Armeeabteilung Hollidt to hold the Chir River, but he only had rear-area troops, Luftwaffe flak units and the remnants of the 22. Panzer-Division, along with some Romanian remnants salvaged by Oberst Walther Wenck. Generaloberst Hermann Hoth was also able to save some Romanian troops and he focused on safeguarding the railhead at Kotelnikovo for the expected reinforcements.

Manstein and his 19-year-old son Gero in mid-October 1942. Two weeks later, Gero was killed in action near Lake Il'men by a Soviet air attack. Gero was serving as an ordnance officer in Manstein's old unit, the 18. Infanterie-Division. (Author's collection)

Once Manstein's headquarters became operational at Novocherkassk (over 200km [125 miles] behind the front) on the morning of 27 November, Heeresgruppe B transferred command over the troops in the Stalingrad *Kessel* to the new Heeresgruppe Don. However, Manstein's headquarters suffered from poor communications with its subordinates units for several days, hindering his efforts to pull the new command together. Manstein's initial orders from the OKH were 'to bring the enemy's attacks to a standstill and recapture the positions previously occupied by us', but once Stalingrad was surrounded, the orders were upgraded to a relief operation to save Paulus' army – which was now about 135km (84 miles) from the new German front line at Kotelnikovo. In his memoirs, Manstein asserted that, 'Sixth Army's subordination to HQ Heeresgruppe Don was more or less a fiction' and he claimed that the OKH and Hitler exercised direct command over Paulus. He added that, 'the army group could no longer command it, but merely give it assistance'. Manstein was aware that the Stalingrad crisis was likely to end badly for the Wehrmacht and he made great efforts to shift blame for what followed to the OKH and Hitler, clearly shirking his command responsibilities.

Although most of the Soviet attention was focused on reducing the Stalingrad *Kessel*, Vatutin assigned General-Major Nikolai Trufanov's 51st Army to defend the south-west approaches to Stalingrad. Despite the Herculean efforts of Hollidt, Hoth and Wenck, Manstein had pitifully little to work with when he first arrived and he doubted whether he could hold the existing front, never mind advance 135km (84 miles) to relieve Paulus.

The OKH promised Manstein reinforcements to mount the relief effort but Hitler was reluctant to shift units from the closest source – Heeresgruppe A in the Caucasus – and agreed only to the transfer of the weak 23. Panzer-Division.

The only experienced and full-strength unit available to mount the relief effort was Generaloberst Erhard Raus' 6. Panzer-Division, en route from Belgium with a full complement of 140 tanks. The lead elements of the 6. Panzer-Division arrived at Kotelnikovo on 27 November. The 11. Panzer-Division also arrived to give Hollidt a mobile reserve on the Chir River front. By early December, Hoth began to form these reinforcements into the XLVIII Panzerkorps and the LVII Panzerkorps. Meanwhile, Manstein's staff developed a rescue plan, Operation *Wintergewitter* (*Winter Storm*), which envisioned a two-pronged offensive with the XLVIII Panzerkorps attacking on the left from the Chir River and the LVII Panzerkorps attacking on the right from Kotelnikovo. However, even if the rescue succeeded in reaching Stalingrad, Manstein knew that Hitler would not authorize the city to be evacuated.

Meanwhile, Vatutin and Yeremenko had no intention of giving Manstein a respite in order to prepare a proper offensive and they sent General-Major Prokofii Romanenko's 5th Tank Army to attack Hollidt's thin line on the Chir River. On 6 December, the 5th Tank Army made a deep penetration across the Chir River, forcing Manstein to commit the XLVIII Panzerkorps to restore the front. Thereafter, the Soviet 5th Tank Army kept up a series of small attacks on the Chir River line that prevented the XLVIII Panzerkorps from participating in *Wintergewitter* and thereby reduced the relief effort to a single corps operation.

Manstein preferred to wait for more reinforcements but Soviet efforts to reduce the Stalingrad *Kessel* indicated that a relief effort must be made before AOK 6 was too weak to break out. Reluctantly, he ordered Hoth to begin Operation *Wintergewitter* on 12 December, with only the 6. and 23. Panzer-Divisionen from LVII Panzerkorps; a total of just 180 tanks. Nevertheless, Hoth's Panzers easily overran Trufanov's two rifle divisions north of Kotelnikovo and the Luftwaffe even managed to scrape up some air support from Fliegerkorps IV. By the end of the first day, Hoth's Panzers had advanced about 20km (12 miles), but Yeremenko quickly sent the 4th Mechanized Corps and 13th Tank Corps to reinforce the wavering 51st Army. On the second day of *Wintergewitter*, Hoth's Panzers reached the Aksay River but Stalin ordered General-Lieutenant Rodion Malinovsky's reinforced 2nd Guards Army to contain the German relief effort.

In a futile race against time, Hoth's Panzers finally succeeded in crossing the Aksay River but then ran straight into the Soviet reinforcements. Raus fought and won a two-day tank battle with the Soviet 4th Mechanized Corps around Verkhne Kumski, but the delay was fatal. Raus succeeded in

Planning a rescue mission

Generalfeldmarschall Erich von Manstein **(1)** conferring with Generaloberst Hermann Hoth **(2)** (commander of 4. Panzerarmee), aboard his command train about the plan to rescue the encircled AOK 6 at Stalingrad, early December 1942. In less than two weeks, Manstein and Hoth were able to plan Operation *Wintergewitter* and assemble a relief force to conduct one of the most desperate German operations of World War II.

1
2

Operation *Wintergewitter* begins on 12 December 1942. Reconnaissance units from the 6. and 23. Panzer-Divisionen begin pushing across the frozen landscape towards Stalingrad. Despite desperate efforts, Hoth's Panzers were unable to rescue the trapped AOK 6 in Stalingrad. (Bundesarchiv, Bild 101I-218-0545-15, Fotograf: Dieck)

slipping a *Kampfgruppe* through to seize a crossing over the Myshkova River – within 48km (30 miles) of the Stalingrad *Kessel* – on the evening of 19 December but they ran into the lead elements of Malinovsky's army, which made any further advance suicidal.

Manstein realized that the relief force was not going to get any closer, but he was reluctant to issue the codeword '*Thunderclap*' initiating a breakout to Paulus, for fear of openly disobeying Hitler. Instead, he sent his Ic (intelligence officer), Major Hans Eismann, into the pocket to convince Paulus to take the initiative on his own. However, Paulus was not the kind of officer to take chances and he asked permission from the OKH to break out, which was refused. Meanwhile, the Soviets began Operation *Malvyy Saturn* (*Little Saturn*) on 16 December, against the Italian 8th Army and Romanian 3rd Army, which pushed in Heeresgruppe Don's left flank. Within a week, Soviet armour was racing towards the Donets and the airbases that supported the Stalingrad airlift. Even worse, the 5th Tank Army got across the Chir River in force and Hollidt could no longer protect Hoth's flanks.

Despite the writing on the wall, Manstein was reluctant to call off *Wintergewitter* while there was still a chance that Hitler might change his mind. For three days he kept Hoth's Panzers on the Myshkova River, vainly hoping to get permission for a breakout or for Paulus to do so on his own. Neither happened. Instead, Malinovsky pounded the stalled Panzer divisions, inflicting serious losses, while the weak Romanian VI and VII Corps guarding Hoth's flanks fell back. By the time Manstein finally called off *Wintergewitter*, virtually his whole front was collapsing and Soviet tanks were overrunning the main Luftwaffe airbase at Tatsinskaya. Worse still, the effort to relieve Stalingrad had badly depleted the LVII Panzerkorps, which was the only mobile reserve available to Heeresgruppe Don. Hoth's forces were so weak that Malinovsky was able to push him all the way back to Kotelnikovo in just five days and by the end of the year, all of Manstein's forces were in retreat.

THE HOUR OF DESTINY

The front collapses, January–February 1943

With AOK 6 written off, Manstein had to focus on building a new southern front on the Donets in order to prevent the Soviets from reaching Rostov, but this was complicated by Hitler's insistence on keeping most of Heeresgruppe A in the Caucasus. Despite the fact that Manstein had only the weak 19. Panzer-Division screening a 60km-wide (37-mile) sector around Starobyelsk after the collapse of the Italians, Hitler was reluctant to give up his bridgehead in the Caucasus when it wasn't under serious attack. Yet as long as Heeresgruppe A remained in the Caucasus, Manstein was forced to keep the 4. Panzerarmee and Armeeabteilung Hollidt tied down protecting their supply lines through Rostov. Thus, Manstein had few forces remaining to deal with his open left flank, which invited a Soviet envelopment. He shuffled his few depleted Panzer divisions about to try and shore up the crumbling front and they succeeded in bruising some of the Soviet spearheads, but even this proved grossly insufficient to break the momentum of the Soviet offensives, which seemed to come one after the other. Raus' once-powerful 6. Panzer-Division was reduced to only 32 tanks by early January, but it was still the best mobile unit left in Heeresgruppe Don. Emboldened by the weakness of Manstein's forces, Vatutin's Southwest Front pushed into the void towards Millerovo and the Donets, forcing the OKH to form Armeeabteilung Fretter-Pico hurriedly in order to delay the steamroller.

It was fortunate for Manstein that AOK 6 held out for another month and tied up seven Soviet armies that would otherwise have been pushing westwards. Nevertheless, a new disaster began on 13 January 1943, when the Bryansk and Voronezh Fronts launched a massive offensive against Heeresgruppe B and quickly overwhelmed the Hungarian 2nd Army. In a week, the Soviets took 89,000 prisoners and the entire Axis front between Orel and Rostov was in a shambles. Heeresgruppe B patched together a screening force from remnants – Armeeabteilung Lanz – to cover the 150km-wide (93-mile) gap between the two army groups. With the entire southern front facing catastrophe Hitler finally authorized part of the 1. Panzerarmee to begin evacuating the Caucasus on 24 January and Manstein promptly directed these three divisions toward his open left flank, which he later referred to in chess terms as 'castling'.

Yet unknown to the Stavka, powerful reinforcements were en route to Manstein's command from Western Europe. SS-Obergruppenführer Paul Hausser's SS-Panzerkorps, with the SS-Panzergrenadier-Divisionen 'Leibstandarte Adolf Hitler', 'Das Reich' and 'Totenkopf', was just beginning to arrive in the Kharkov area in late January. Hausser's corps had 317 tanks, which made it one of the most powerful armoured formations on the Eastern Front. However, Hitler rightly considered this corps to be a strategic asset and he insisted that it would remain under direct OKH control and that Manstein could not use it without permission.

With Armeeabteilung Hollidt retreating towards Rostov, Manstein was forced to abandon his headquarters at Novocherkassk and relocate to Zaporozhe. Stalin ordered the Red Army to press its advantage and the Stavka decided that it was time to put the theory of 'deep operations' into practice. Although Soviet forces were

In early January 1943, Heeresgruppe Don received 29 Tiger tanks in schwere-Panzer-Abteilung 503, but instead of committing them to reinforce Manstein's crumbling left flank, they were sent to assist 1. Panzerarmee's withdrawal to Rostov. By the time they returned to Manstein's control, only a handful of Tigers were still operational. Many of those immobilized by mechanical defects, like this one, had to be blown up during the retreat. (Nik Cornish, WH 916)

depleted and logistic support was inadequate, the Stavka assessed that Heeresgruppe B and Heeresgruppe Don were disintegrating and decided to mount two major offensives to prevent the Germans from establishing a new front east of the Dnepr River. On 29–30 January, Vatutin's Southwest Front would begin operation *Skachok* (*Gallop*) by attacking Manstein's weak left flank. Once a penetration of the thin German defence line was achieved, Vatutin would push Mobile Group Popov, which had over 200 tanks in four tank corps, southwards 300km (186 miles) to the Sea of Azov to cut off Heeresgruppe Don. Even though most front-line Soviet units were down to about 60 per cent strength, they still began these new offensives with a two to one numerical advantage in manpower and a four to one superiority in armour. On 2 February, General-Colonel Filipp I. Golikov's Voronezh Front would begin Operation *Zvezda* (*Star*) with three armies advancing on Kharkov and two armies toward Kursk. Malinovsky's Southern Front would continue to push slowly toward Rostov to pin Heeresgruppe Don, while Golikov and Vatutin advanced into the gap between Heeresgruppe B and Heeresgruppe Don.

Initially, the twin Soviet offensives went well and the Germans were forced to give up a great deal of ground, albeit slowly. On Vatutin's front, the 1st Guards Army succeeded in crossing the Donets River on 1 February, but then ran straight into III Panzerkorps at Slavyansk. Vatutin was surprised to find that reinforcements from 1. Panzerarmee had already arrived in Manstein's command, but rather than going around this obstacle, he began a two-week battle for these towns. When the tired Soviet rifle divisions proved too weak to gain a breakthrough on their own, Vatutin foolishly committed part of Mobile Group Popov – intended for exploitation – to overwhelm the German strongpoint at Slavyansk. Popov managed to encircle the 7. Panzer-Division for a time, but this slugfest consumed Vatutin's limited supplies of fuel and ammunition and diverted him from his true operational objectives. Meanwhile, Manstein prodded 1. Panzerarmee to rush its XL Panzerkorps to reinforce III Panzerkorps at Slavyansk. It was not until 11 February that Vatutin came to his senses and decided to remove Popov's armour from the inconclusive fight at Slavyansk and send it around 1. Panzerarmee's open left flank. Utilizing the superb mobility of their tanks to the fullest, the 4th Guards Tank Corps advanced over 50km (30 miles) through deep snow and surprised the Germans by occupying Krasnoarmeyskoye, thereby severing Heeresgruppe Don's main line of railway communications back to Dnepropetrovsk. When Vatutin realized that there were virtually no Germans defending a 100km-wide (62-mile) gap between 1. Panzerarmee and the SS-Panzerkorps, he finally energized the 6th Army and the rest of Popov's armour to push toward Pavlograd and the Dnepr River. Unless decisive action was taken quickly, Vatutin's forces would soon isolate Heeresgruppe Don.

On Golikov's Voronezh Front, Operation *Zvezda* succeeded in pushing back Armeeabteilung Lanz,[1] and in desperation Lanz began committing parts

1. Renamed Armeeabteilung Kempf on 21 February when Lanz was relieved of command for the loss of Kharkov.

The crisis of Heeresgruppe Don, 19 December 1942–1 February 1943

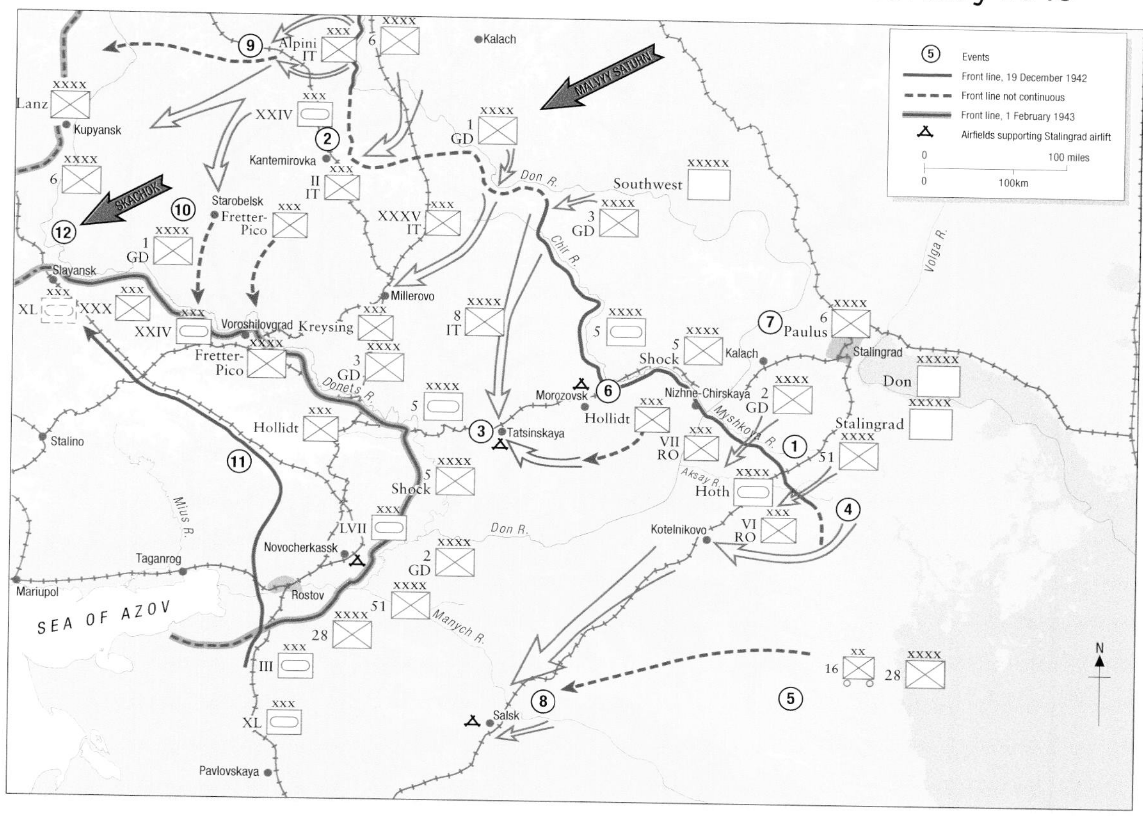

1. 19 December: Hoth's Panzers reach the Myshkova River, but can advance no further. Paulus opts not to attempt a breakout from the Stalingrad pocket.
2. 19 December: Operation Malvyy Saturn (Little Saturn), which began on 16 December, continues to demolish the Italian Eighth Army. Kantemirovka falls.
3. 24 December: Soviet tanks overrun the airfield at Tatsinskaya, severely disrupting the airlift to Stalingrad.
4. 24 December: the Stalingrad Front's 51st and 2nd Guard Armies begin pushing Hoth's Panzers back from the Myshkova River. Both Romanian corps guarding Hoth's flanks disintegrate in a matter of days, forcing him to fall back to Kotelnikovo.
5. 30 December: the 16. Infanterie-Division (mot), responsible for screening the open Kalmyuk steppe, begins to retreat. The Soviet 28th Army pursues.
6. 2 January: the airfield at Morozovsk is captured, which also severs the rail line to Armeeabteilung Hollidt. Hollidt orders a withdrawal back to the Donets.
7. 10 January: the Don Front begins Operation *Koltso* (*Ring*) to reduce AOK 6 in the Stalingrad pocket. Fighting continues for three weeks, until Paulus surrenders.
8. 11 January: the Soviet 51st Army and 2nd Guards Army reach the Manych River, threatening the rear of Heeresgruppe A in the Caucasus.
9. 13 January: the Soviet 6th Army attacks and isolates the Italian Alpini corps. After desperate fighting, the Italian survivors succeed in breaking out and reaching the Donets.
10. 24 January: the 6th Army captures Starobyelsk. Both the XXIV Panzerkorps and Armeeabteilung Fretter-Pico withdraw south of the Donets.
11. 24 January: once Hitler finally authorizes 1. Panzerarmee to withdraw from the Caucasus to support Manstein's defence on the Donets, Manstein promptly sends III and XL Panzerkorps to plug the hole in his line around Slavyansk.
12. 29–30 January: Vatutin's Southwest Front begins Operation *Skachok* (Gallop) by attacking Manstein's weak left flank on the Donets. The 6th Army does not cross the Donets until 1 February.

of the newly arrived 2. SS-Panzergrenadier-Division 'Das Reich' to set up blocking positions position east of Kharkov. Hitler objected to this piecemeal commitment of the SS-Panzerkorps but this act succeeded in buying vital time for the rest of the 'Das Reich' and 'Leibstandarte' divisions to arrive in Kharkov. Indeed, 'Das Reich' repulsed every effort by the 3rd Tank Army to cross the

Donets River between 5 and 9 February. Meanwhile, Manstein flew to meet Hitler at the Wolfsschanze in Rastenberg on 6 February to iron out priorities for dealing with the two Soviet offensives. Although Manstein was more worried about Vatutin's breakthrough, Hitler was only concerned with Kharkov, which he dictated be held at all costs. Manstein finally convinced Hitler that in order to gain the reserves needed to mount a real counteroffensive, he would have to shorten his line by giving up Rostov. Hitler reluctantly authorized Armeeabteilung Hollidt to retreat over 120km (75 miles) back to the Mius River, where it could form a stronger defensive line. He also gave Manstein permission to shift Hoth's 4. Panzerarmee from the Rostov area to stop Vatutin's drive toward the Dnepr. Thus, the 6 February conference finally gave Manstein the flexibility that he needed to conduct his kind of *Bewegungskrieg*, rather than just positional warfare reacting to Soviet offensives.

While Hitler and Manstein were deciding the operational context for the German counterblow, Lanz and Hausser conducted a dogged but futile defence of Kharkov. Hausser held the approaches to the city with his two divisions, reinforced by the Infanterie-Division 'Großdeutschland' (mot.), but Golikov was approaching with three armies. Golikov began a frontal assault upon Kharkov with the 69th Army and 3rd Tank Army on 10 February but Hausser repulsed these attacks. However, the retreat of Armeeabteilung Lanz from Belgorod left no continuous German defence north of Kharkov and Golikov sent the 40th Army, to envelop the city. Even worse, the Soviet 6th Guards Cavalry Corps moved into an undefended area south of Kharkov and threatened to sever the only remaining rail line into the city. Lanz only had enough reserves to deal with one threat at a time and he chose to eliminate the Soviet cavalry, but this weakened the defence of the city at a critical moment. By 14 February, Rybalko's 3rd Tank Army reached the eastern outskirts of Kharkov and the Soviet 40th Army was enveloping the city from the north-west. On that day, Hitler gave Manstein command over both Armeeabteilung Lanz and the SS-Panzerkorps. Based on Hitler's promises

Panzers from the 'Leibstandarte's Kampfgruppe Witte pause on the outskirts of Kharkov, 11 March 1943. Manstein's rapid recapture of the city and rout of the Soviet Southwest and Voronezh Fronts earned him further prestige with Hitler. (Bundesarchiv, Bild 101III-Cantzler-067-14, Fotograf: Cantzler)

of more reinforcements, Manstein ordered Lanz and Hausser to hold Kharkov at all costs. However, Hausser recognized that his corps was in danger of encirclement and he immediately requested permission to withdraw from the city, which Manstein refused. With the trap about to close, Hausser decided to evacuate Kharkov in direct disobedience of Hitler's order to hold the city at all costs. Manstein radioed Hausser to hold Kharkov but, confusingly, told him to avoid encirclement. Manstein clearly didn't want to lose the bulk of the SS-Panzerkorps in a hopeless battle to save a prestige objective, but as with Paulus at Stalingrad, he lacked the moral courage required of higher commanders and left it up to his subordinates to risk their own necks when tough calls had to be made. After heavy fighting, Golikov's forces fought their way into Kharkov by noon on 16 February, but the Großdeutschland Division and the SS-Panzerkorps escaped to fight another day. Nevertheless, both the 'Leibstandarte' and 'Das Reich' suffered heavy losses in the Kharkov fighting and only one-third of their Panzers were still operational.

Generalfeldmarschall von Manstein greets Hitler at Zaporozhe on March 18, 1943. Hitler was grateful to Manstein for stabilizing the front and recovering Kharkov. (Bundesarchiv, Bild 146-1995-041-23A)

Enraged by the loss of Kharkov, Hitler flew to Manstein's headquarters at Zaporozhe on 17 February to find out why his orders had been disobeyed. Manstein was aware that his career, along with those of Hausser and Lanz, was on the line and according to Josef Goebbels, Hitler was prepared to relieve Manstein for the loss of Kharkov. Instead, Manstein deftly managed to shift blame onto Lanz and Hausser and Hitler was satisfied with replacing Lanz with Werner Kempf. Hitler also wanted Manstein to make the recapture of Kharkov the main priority for the upcoming counteroffensive, but Manstein successfully pointed out the more serious danger posed by Vatutin's advance towards the supply lines over the Dnepr. Reinforcing Manstein's case, Soviet tanks from Mobile Group Popov approached to within 32km (20 miles) of the Dnepr River on the day of Hitler's arrival. When the Führer saw on the situation maps that there were virtually no German units in their path to prevent them from severing the main supply networks across the Dnepr in the next few days, he finally realized the gravity of the situation. Hitler agreed that Manstein could use the SS-Panzerkorps first to stop Vatutin, then to recover Kharkov. Given the disintegration of virtually all of Heeresgruppe B's constituent formations, Hitler decided to dissolve that headquarters and to redesignate Manstein's command as Heeresgruppe Süd, effective immediately. Thus, Manstein was now responsible for stopping both operations *Zvezda* and *Shackok*, each of which seemed to be on the verge of achieving decisive success. For Manstein, the hour of destiny in his military career had now arrived and it would require every bit of his professional skill to stave off a catastrophe.

Kharkov 1943: the backhand blow

Manstein had been preparing for a counteroffensive throughout February, but in order to mass sufficient forces for a credible strike, he had to accept risk in some areas. Once behind the Mius River, Hollidt's group was able to secure Heeresgruppe Süd's right flank for the time being. Heeresgruppe Süd was also beginning to receive some fresh infantry divisions from Western Europe, which freed the Panzer divisions from front-line defence duty. Yet even after the arrival of 1. Panzerarmee, Manstein's left flank still had a huge gap between it and Armeeabteilung Kempf – into which Popov's armour and the Soviet 6th Army were advancing. Manstein's planned a classic *Bewegungskrieg* solution – a concentric pincer attack with fast-moving formations to cut off and destroy the Soviet penetration. By capturing Kharkov, the Soviets actually facilitated Manstein's plan by releasing the SS-Panzerkorps from a fixed defence of that city. Manstein now ordered Hausser to concentrate his corps near Krasnograd and prepare for a counterattack. To block the approaches to the Dnepr River, Manstein shifted XLVIII Panzerkorps from Hoth's 4. Panzerarmee to Dnepropetrovsk. Hoth would be in charge of the main effort, consisting of the SS-Panzerkorps and XLVIII Panzerkorps, while Mackensen's 1. Panzerarmee would launch a supporting attack with XL and LVII Panzerkorps.

On the other side of the hill, Vatutin reported to the Stavka that, 'without a doubt, the enemy is hurrying to withdraw his forces from the Donbas [Donets Basin] across the Dnepr'. Soviet intelligence detected Manstein concentrating Panzer units, but misinterpreted them as indicators of a German evacuation. Vatutin mistakenly concluded that the Germans were on the run and he pushed his forces past the culmination point where they were effective. While it was true that the 25th Tank Corps was within 32km (20 miles) of the Dnepr River, it was virtually out of fuel and Mobile Group Popov was spread out, rather than concentrated. Golikov also decided to push his 40th and 69th Armies further westwards after capturing Kharkov, but this simply dispersed the exhausted Voronezh Front even further. Armeeabteilung Kempf slowly fell back under pressure and Kempf begged for reinforcements to prevent

OPPOSITE

1. 19 February: Manstein boldly orders the 15. Infanterie-Division to detrain just outside Sinel'nikovo. This move catches the Soviet 25th Tank Corps by surprise and the town is recaptured.
2. 19 February: XL Panzerkorps defeats the Soviet 4th Guards Tank Corps at Krasnoarmeyskoye.
3. 20 February: 2. SS-Panzergrenadier-Division 'Das Reich' and 3. SS-Panzergrenadier-Division 'Totenkopf' begin attacking into the flank of the Soviet 6th Army near Pavlograd.
4. 21 February: XLVIII Panzerkorps begins attacking north towards Lozovaya.
5. 23–24 February: XL Panzerkorps (5. SS-Panzergrenadier-Division 'Wiking', 7. and 11. Panzer-Divisionen) rolls up Popov's three stranded tank corps north of Krasnoarmeyskoye.
6. 25–26 February: the battle of Lozovaya. The SS-Panzerkorps and XLVIII Panzerkorps envelop the town and, after heavy fighting, crush the trapped defenders.
7. 20–28 February: the Soviet 40th and 69th Armies continue to advance westward, pushing back Armeeabteilung Kempf. Golikov shifts to the defence once it is clear that Vatutin has been defeated.
8. 3–5 March: the Stavka orders Rybalko's 3rd Guards Tank Army to move south to stop the 4. Panzerarmee drive on Kharkov, but the SS-Panzerkorps encircles and destroys Rybalko's armour.
9. 6 March: Hoth shifts the SS-Panzerkorps and XLVIII Panzerkorps westwards and begins the advance on Kharkov, with six mechanized divisions on line.
10. 7 March: Korps Raus begins a supporting attack against the 69th Army, which begins to withdraw.
11. 10–14 March: the Third battle of Kharkov. The SS-Panzerkorps succeeds in enveloping the city to the north, but XLVIII Panzerkorps lacks the strength to complete the encirclement. The SS-Panzerkorps fights its way into the city against fierce resistance.

The 'backhand blow' – the third battle of Kharkov, February–March 1943

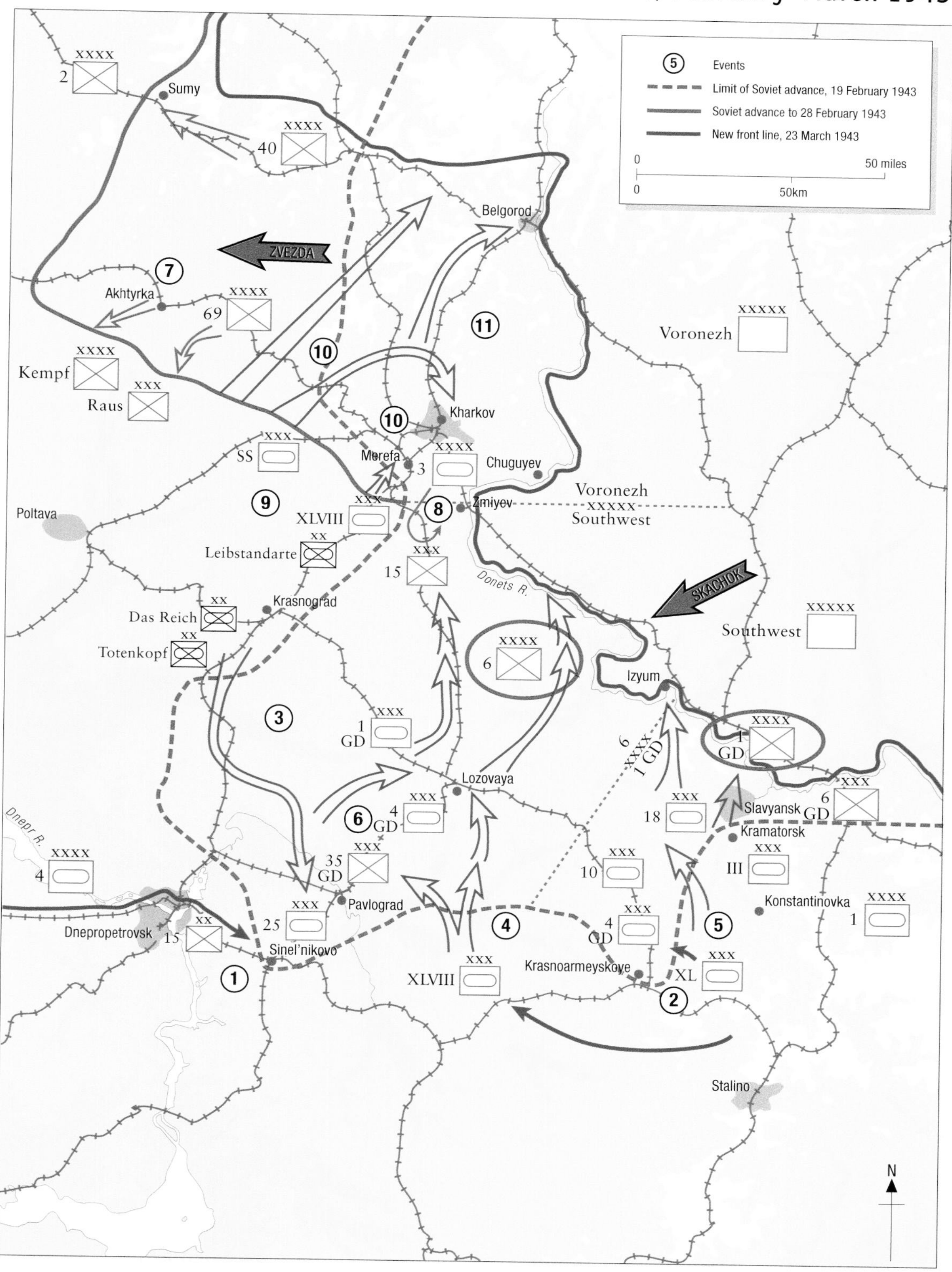

a complete collapse. Manstein knew that he lacked the resources to both help Kempf and mount a counteroffensive, so he told Kempf that he could expect no further help until the counteroffensive had achieved its objectives. Although Manstein was aware that Kempf lacked the forces to maintain a continuous front, he took the calculated risk that his own counteroffensive would succeed before Golikov could destroy Armeeabteilung Kempf.

Manstein took another calculated risk by ordering the lead elements of the 15. Infanterie-Division – just arriving by rail from France – to detrain on the outskirts of Sinel'nikovo, which the Soviet 25th Tank Corps had occupied. The infantrymen succeeded in bringing in a regimental-sized *Kampfgruppe* before the Soviets could react and they proceeded to push the surprised Soviet tankers out of the town on 19 February. By seizing Sinel'nikovo, Manstein placed a fresh blocking force between the Soviet spearheads and the Dnepr River, so Hoth could now focus on collapsing the flanks of the Soviet penetration. In another preliminary operation, XL Panzerkorps isolated and defeated the Soviet 4th Guards Tank Corps at Krasnoarmeyskoye, which helped to clear the rail line to keep Armeeabteilung Hollidt in supply.

Hoth began the counteroffensive early on the morning of 20 February. While leaving the SS-Panzergrenadier-Division 'Leibstandarte SS Adolf Hitler' to help delay Golikov's advance west from Kharkov, the rest of Hausser's SS-Panzerkorps struck south from Krasnograd into the flank of the 6th Army. Initially only the SS-Panzergrenadier-Division 'Das Reich' attacked with 56 tanks and assault guns, but SS-Panzergrenadier-Division 'Totenkopf' joined in two days later with another 90 tanks. The XLVIII Panzerkorps, with 6. and 17. Panzer-Divisionen, began attacking north towards Lozovaya. The ground was frozen enough for the German armoured *Kampfgruppen* to advance over 100km (62 miles) in three days, but after that an early spring thaw produced thick mud that reduced German mobility. Vatutin remained oblivious to the threat and ordered the 6th Army to conduct a river crossing of the Dnepr River on the night of 21–22 February but instead, the SS-Panzergrenadier-Division 'Das Reich' isolated part of the 6th Army and recaptured Pavlograd on 22 February. The next day, XL Panzerkorps joined the counteroffensive on the right of XLVIII Panzerkorps. At this point, Vatutin finally recognized the threat and began trying to shift reserves to deal with the enemy counteroffensive and he asked the Stavka to have Golikov suspend his westward advance.

Manstein's counteroffensive gathered momentum on 24 February, as XL Panzerkorps rolled up Popov's three isolated tank corps, each of which had been reduced to a few dozen tanks. The three German *Panzerkorps* simply destroyed Vatutin's forces piecemeal before they could react, although they did put up a tough fight in the town of Lozovaya. Vatutin never issued orders to shift to a defence, so the Germans caught many units still strung out and dispersed. The Luftwaffe also reappeared and helped to smash up Soviet troop concentrations. After the capture of Lozovaya, Hoth shifted the SS-Panzerkorps' axis of advance north towards Kharkov, while XL and XLVIII Panzerkorps pushed Vatutin's forces back to the north-east. Even though XLVIII Panzerkorps was down to only eight operational tanks between its two Panzer divisions, the Soviet 6th Army and 1st Guards Army were in full retreat back to the Donets and put up only minimal resistance. Despite Vatutin committing the remaining reserves from the Voronezh Front to try and hold his one toehold across the Donets at Slavyansk, the 1st Guards Army was forced to retreat across the river.

While Manstein was demolishing Vatutin's command, Golikov continued to push back Armeeabteilung Kempf. However, once the Stavka realized the threat to the Southwest Front, it ordered Golikov to suspend his offensive and send Rybalko's 3rd Tank Army to support Vatutin's hard-pressed forces. It was a case of too little and too late, since Rybalko's army had barely 30 tanks left and by the time that it arrived Vatutin's forces were already in full retreat. Rybalko moved south from Kharkov on 3 March and ran straight into the SS-Panzerkorps, which quickly smashed his armour to pieces. By 5 March, Rybalko had no tanks left but he still had three rifle divisions and the 6th Guards Cavalry Corps to protect the southern approaches to Kharkov. To replace his losses, the Stavka managed to send Rybalko two more tank brigades and more infantry, but the battlefield initiative had passed to the Germans.

The defeat of 3rd Tank Army's mobile units provided the perfect lead-in for the second phase of Manstein's counteroffensive, in which he intended to encircle and destroy the bulk of Golikov's Voronezh Front. Golikov placed the 40th and 69th Armies to defend Kharkov but he had occupied far more ground than his depleted rifle divisions could hold and he no longer had an armoured reserve. Manstein designated the 4. Panzerarmee with all three divisions from the SS-Panzerkorps as his main effort, supported on their right by three Panzer divisions from XLVIII Panzerkorps. Hausser began his attack on 6 March and made rapid progress towards Kharkov against three rifle divisions from the 69th Army. On 7 March, Armeeabteilung Kempf joined the counteroffensive by attacking the over-extended 40th Army with the Infanterie-Division 'Großdeutschland' (mot.) and two infantry divisions. Within three days, the Waffen-SS troops were on the outskirts of Kharkov and by 10 March they were enveloping the city to the north. Manstein preferred to encircle the city and avoid costly urban combat, but an impatient Hitler spurred Hausser to finish off the defenders quickly and he ordered the SS-Panzergrenadier-Division 'Leibstandarte' to fight its way into the city. After heavy urban combat, Hausser's SS troops secured Kharkov on 14 March and succeeded in pushing Golikov's troops all the way back to the Donets. In one last spasm, Hausser's troops reoccupied Belgorod on 16 March but the Infanterie-Division Großdeutschland (mot.) bumped into three full-strength Soviet tanks corps that had been rushed to the area by the Stavka, indicating that the days of smashing weak, unsupplied formations were over. Manstein had hoped to continue on to seize Kursk, but now that Soviet reinforcements were appearing in great numbers and the roads were turning into muddy quagmires, he decided to quit while he was ahead. The SS-Panzerkorps had suffered 11,519 casualties in the counteroffensive and was reduced to barely

100 operational tanks and assault guns. The XLVIII Panzerkorps was in even worse shape, with only about 40 tanks still operational.

All told, Manstein's month-long counteroffensive had completely defeated Vatutin's front and severely battered Golikov's front. Vatutin's command had suffered about 30,000 casualties and Golikov's 58,000 casualties, as well as significant material losses. Although the haul of prisoners by 4. Panzerarmee was small by earlier standards – Hoth claimed 12,430 were captured – Manstein's counteroffensive had succeeded in mauling eight of the 20 Soviet tank corps on the Eastern Front. While none of these corps were destroyed, virtually all of them required three to four months to rebuild and recover, which gave the Wehrmacht vital breathing space. The only substantial gain that the Soviets managed to retain from either *Zvezda* or *Skachok* was the Kursk salient, which jutted into the boundary between Heeresgruppe Süd and Heeresgruppe Mitte. Manstein's counteroffensive brought the string of Soviet victories to a sudden, ignominious end and restored some hope to the Wehrmacht. Despite defeat at Stalingrad, Manstein's victory demonstrated that the Wehrmacht could still conduct successful *Bewegungskrieg* – albeit on a limited scale and under favourable circumstances.

Operation *Zitadelle*

The spring thaw gave both sides time to rebuild and to ponder their next move. Manstein realized that despite the success of his 'backhand blow', Heeresgruppe Süd was still very weak and would have difficulty containing another full-scale Soviet offensive. Hitler was grateful that Manstein had recovered Kharkov and restored the front, but he rejected a defensive strategy and sought to regain the initiative in 1943 by launching a limited-objectives offensive in a location where the odds of German success were favourable.

Kessel! German troops encircle and destroy Soviet armour in February 1943

As part of Operation *Gallop*, Vatutin's Southwest Front committed Mobile Group Popov, with four tank corps, to sever Heeresgruppe Don's supply lines and to reach the Dnepr River. They nearly did it, but ran out of fuel before they reached their objectives. On the morning of 20 February 1943, Manstein began his counteroffensive, relying on speed to surround and encircle Popov's four stranded tank corps between Krasnoarmeyskoye and Stepanovka. In just three days of fighting, the XL Panzerkorps overwhelmed one Soviet tank corps after another, until Popov's command was destroyed. Although the Germans lacked the infantry to properly seal off these *Kessel* and many Soviet troops escaped, they were forced to abandon all their equipment. Here, a mixed *Kampfgruppe* from the 7. Panzer-Division has surrounded part of the Soviet 10th Tank Corps. Two German PzKpfw IVF2 tanks establish a hasty blocking position with a few *Panzergrenadiere*, while a mobile flak unit forms another blocking unit on their left flank. Lacking fuel and ammunition, the Soviet tankers can no longer put up effective resistance; a few surrender, but most escape on foot to the woods in the distance. Manstein's *Kessel* tactics did not require large armoured forces but instead relied on speed and efficient coordination to literally run rings around their stronger opponents.

Manstein recommended the elimination of the Kursk salient as a logical continuation of his March counteroffensive and argued that success there would be a major setback for the Red Army. When Manstein made his initial proposal for an attack on the Kursk salient in late March, the Voronezh Front was still reeling from its losses around Kharkov and it seemed ripe for the picking. The OKH agreed to Manstein's proposal, but it was Generaloberst Kurt Zeitzler, chief of the Generalstab, who actually developed the plan for Operation *Zitadelle*. Zeitzler's plan for *Zitadelle* required Manstein's Heeresgruppe Süd to launch a massive pincer attack on the Kursk salient in conjunction with Generalfeldmarschall Günther von Kluge's Heeresgruppe Mitte as 'soon as the weather permits'. Ideally, the two army groups would meet at Kursk, trapping perhaps five to six Soviet armies in the giant *Kessel*. Thus, Manstein had a great influence upon German strategic choices made in 1943 and bears considerable responsibility for *Zitadelle*.

However, Hitler shifted back to one of his risk-averse moods after Stalingrad and he wanted the German summer offensive of 1943 to be a sure thing, not some jury-rigged attack like the March battles. Heinz Guderian, now inspector of Panzer troops, advised against *Zitadelle* and suggested that it could bleed Germany's last reserves dry. A worried Hitler decided on 30 April to delay *Zitadelle* until the Panzer units committed to the offensive could be further strengthened, although this also gave the Soviets time to rebuild their depleted forces, as well.

Instead, it was not until 5 July 1943 that Hitler finally decided to launch *Zitadelle,* by which point the operation had grown from a limited counteroffensive to one that involved 60 per cent of all the German armour on the Eastern Front. The mission assigned to Manstein's Heeresgruppe Süd in *Zitadelle* was to penetrate that part of the Voronezh Front (now under Vatutin) held by the 6th Guards Army and advance due north towards Oboyan. The ultimate objective, Kursk, lay some 120km (75 miles) from the German start line. At Kursk, Manstein's forces would link up with Generaloberst Walter Model's AOK 9 advancing south from the Orel salient. Manstein made Hoth's 4. Panzerarmee his main effort, with XLVIII Panzerkorps on the left and Hausser's II SS-Panzerkorps on the right. After three months of rebuilding, these two corps began the offensive with 925 tanks and 170 assault guns, which made Hoth's 4. Panzerarmee the strongest German armoured strike force ever assembled in the Soviet Union. Manstein also directed Armeeabteilung Kempf to make a supporting attack on 4. Panzerarmee's right flank to widen the initial breach and to counter the expected reaction of the Soviet armoured reserves. Kempf committed III Panzerkorps with 369 tanks and assault guns to this supporting attack against the Soviet 7th Guard Army. Manstein knew that *Zitadelle* was going to be a much tougher fight than the March battles, particularly since his three attacking corps would have to penetrate three heavily fortified belts held by full-strength guards units then deal with counterattacks by one or more Soviet tank armies. In order to give his assault units all possible advantages, he used his experience in dealing with Soviet fortified belts at Sevastopol to provide lavish artillery and engineer support.

Fliegerkorps VIII was also expected to help pin down Soviet reserves and to disrupt enemy troop concentrations, as it had in previous offensives.

Soviet anti-tank gunners firing point-blank at a German StuG III assault gun during the battle of Kursk in July 1943. Manstein's forces bent, but could not break Vatutin's defences. The days of easy victories for the Panzers were over. (RIA Novosti, 288)

Initially, Manstein committed only 14 of the 42 divisions in Heeresgruppe Süd to the *Zitadelle* offensive. Armeeabteilung Hollidt, renamed as the new AOK 6, continued to hold the Mius River line with 12 divisions, while Generaloberst Eberhard von Mackensen's 1. Panzerarmee held the Donets River front with 11 divisions. In order to conduct *Zitadelle,* Manstein had to concentrate 85 per cent of his available armour on a narrow, 50km-wide (31-mile) attack front, while Hollidt and Mackensen defended more than 200km (120 miles) of front with minimal armour support. Manstein had got away with this type of risk in 1942 when the Soviets were spread thinly themselves, but now he was slow to realize that the Red Army of 1943 had transformed itself into a much more capable force.

After a preliminary attack on 4 July to clear away the 6th Guards Army's combat outposts, Hoth's 4. Panzerarmee began its main attack at 0400hrs on 5 July. Manstein was expecting most of the assault divisions to reach the Soviet second line of defence near the Psel River – up to 45km (28 miles) north of the start line – by the end of the first day, based upon the ability of Panzer divisions to breach Soviet fortified lines in the past. However, the furthest advance achieved by XLVIII Panzerkorps on the first day was only 5km (3 miles) and it failed to penetrate the Soviet first defensive line. In the centre, Hausser's II SS-Panzerkorps succeeded in penetrating the first defensive line and advanced up to 20km (12 miles), but with heavy casualties. On the right, III Panzerkorps made minor advances of 3–6km (2–4 miles) against the 7th Guards Army. Manstein and Hoth were shocked by the difficulty experienced on the first day, since the Panzers had never failed to achieve a breakthrough. Without a doubt, the Soviets had massed anti-tank defences, minefields, artillery and infantry fieldworks in sufficient densities to take the stride out of Manstein's style of *Bewegungskrieg*.

Hoth and Kempf continued their attacks on 6 July but it was soon clear that Heeresgruppe Süd was involved in a costly battle of attrition rather than the free-ranging manoeuvre warfare that Manstein preferred. Hausser's II SS-Panzerkorps continued to grind forwards, but XLVIII Panzerkorps had considerable difficulty on the left flank and by the time it got within 26km (16 miles) of Oboyan on 9 July its strength was nearly spent. By the same date, Kempf's attack had also run out of steam and it failed to protect the right flank of Hausser's corps. Kempf's attack did force Vatutin to commit the 1st Tank Army prematurely and the Stavka decided to bring up the 5th Guards Tank Army and 5th Guards Army to stop Hoth's advance once and for all. In response, Manstein transferred XXIV Panzerkorps from 1. Panzerarmee to reinforce Hoth's faltering attack. However, it was already clear that *Zitadelle* had failed, since Model's AOK 9 was unable to achieve a penetration north of Kursk and shifted to a defensive posture. Hoth made one last effort to batter his way through at Prokhorovka on 12 July and succeeded in defeating the 5th Guards Tank Army, but 4. Panzerarmee was spent.

Hitler summoned Manstein and Kluge to Rastenberg on the day after Prokhorovka to announce that he was suspending *Zitadelle*. Manstein was adamant that his offensive continue, saying 'victory on the southern front of the Kursk salient is within reach. The enemy has thrown in nearly his entire strategic reserves and is badly mauled. Breaking off action now would be throwing away victory.' However, Hitler realized that the offensive no longer had any chance of encircling large Soviet formations and that it was only grinding up the Wehrmacht's precious armoured reserves in a useless battle of attrition. Hitler directed Manstein to transfer 1. SS-Panzergrenadier-Division 'Leibstandarte SS Adolf Hitler' to Italy in response to the Allied landing on Sicily on 10 July and authorized Heeresgruppe Süd to fall back to the defensive positions it held at the start of *Zitadelle*.

Manstein's forces had suffered 29,102 casualties during the offensive, including 4,759 killed. Although Heeresgruppe Süd reported only 190 tanks as total losses during the offensive, less than half its armour was operational by 15 July. Vatutin's Voronezh Front and reinforcements from Steppe Front had suffered over 90,000 casualties, including 18,097 killed. Soviet armour losses in this sector were 1,254 tanks out of 2,924 committed. While Manstein had succeeded in inflicting better than three to one losses on Vatutin's front and advancing a maximum of 38km (24 miles), he had failed to achieve his operational objective of encircling any enemy units.

Retreat to the Dnepr

Once the great offensive was called off, Manstein later wrote that he 'hoped to have given the enemy so much punishment in the course of *Zitadelle* that we could now count on a breathing space in this part of the front'. However, on 17 July the Soviets began probing attacks along the Donets and Mius rivers that gained small bridgeheads. Hollidt's forces were hard pressed and he failed to prevent two Soviet mechanized corps from crossing the Mius. Unable to penetrate the dense Soviet defences around Kursk, Manstein now saw these small Soviet offensives as a perfect opportunity to conduct another 'backhand blow' that might redeem the failure of *Zitadelle*. However, in his eagerness to pull off another *Bewegungskrieg* coup, Manstein made the fatal mistake of underestimating his opponent. Believing that Vatutin's force were no longer an immediate threat after *Zitadelle,* Manstein dispatched the two remaining divisions of II SS-Panzerkorps, along with III and XXIV Panzerkorps, to crush the Mius River crossings. Thus by late July, Manstein had shifted most of his armour southwards but he failed to realize that these probing attacks were diversions intended to draw his attention away from the critical Belgorod–Kharkov sector. In his memoirs, Manstein admitted that this decision proved to be 'disastrous,' but crassly blamed it on Hitler's insistence on holding the Donets Basin.

After repulsing the Soviet breakthrough at Izyum, Hausser's II SS-Panzerkorps attacked the Soviet bridgehead across the Mius River on 30 July. Amazingly, Hausser ran into the same kind of lethal anti-tank defences encountered at Kursk and lost more than 70 tanks on the first day. Hausser only succeeded in eliminating the Soviet bridgehead and capturing 18,000 prisoners after three days of heavy fighting. Although this was a tactical success, it came at a heavy cost since the II SS-Panzerkorps was reduced to fewer than 70 operational tanks and assault guns.

German anti-tank units exacted a heavy toll on enemy armour but could not stop the Red Army's drive to the Dnepr River in September 1943. Here, an 88mm Pak 43/41 anti-tank gun waits in ambush. (Bundesarchiv, Bild 101I-705-0270-18, Fotograf: Bauer-Altvater)

Unnoticed by Manstein's staff, Vatutin had quickly replaced his losses after *Zitadelle* and massed over 800 tanks from the 1st Tank Army and the 5th Guards Tank Army in a narrow 12km (7-mile) sector north-west of Belgorod, near the boundary between 4. Panzerarmee and Armeeabteilung Kempf. Marshal Georgiy Zhukov and the Stavka began preparing Operation *Rumantsyev* even before *Zitadelle* ended and they provided Vatutin with an overwhelming force to recapture Kharkov and press on to the Dnepr River. Zhukov wanted no amateurish offensive this time, but a well-planned and well-supported operation that minimized the risk from any 'backhand blows' from Manstein. The offensive began on 3 August with a massive two-hour artillery preparation against 4. Panzerarmee's LII Armeekorps. In order to conduct the counterattack on the Mius, Manstein had reduced Hoth's army to only four infantry and three Panzer divisions and the Soviet 5th Guards Army was able to rapidly punch through Hoth's weak defences. Vatutin then committed two tank armies into the gap and Hoth's depleted Panzer divisions could not stop the onslaught. By nightfall on the first day, Vatutin's spearheads had advanced up to 26km (16 miles). Vatutin also put heavy pressure on Armeeabteilung Kempf's positions north of Belgorod with attacks from the 53rd and 69th Armies.

Manstein was stunned by the intensity of Vatutin's offensive, which smashed three infantry divisions on the first day. He ordered the III Panzerkorps and the 2. SS-Panzergrenadier-Division 'Das Reich' to return from the Izyum sector, but before they arrived the Soviet 69th Army captured Belgorod on 5 August and the 6th Guards Army eliminated 7,000 German troops in the Borisovka Pocket. The defeated remnants of Hoth's 4. Panzerarmee retreated westwards down the Vorskla River valley, leaving a wide undefended gap between it and Armeeabteilung Kempf. It was not until 7 August that Panzer units from the Mius front began to arrive in Kharkov, by which point the 5th Guards Tank Army's spearheads were within 25km (16 miles) of the city. Between 8 and 12 August, Hoth and Kempf managed to re-establish a line of sorts, but these measures only slowed Vatutin's advance. Just when Manstein thought that he might be able to get the situation under control, the Soviet Southwest Front attacked 1. Panzerarmee in the Donbas and the South Front attacked AOK 6 on the Mius. Both attacks were powerful and quickly gained ground, since both armies had transferred their armour northwards to save Kharkov. Manstein was now faced with simultaneous heavy Soviet attacks against all four of his armies and all his reserves were committed. Rather than wasting time shifting armour back to the Mius front, he kept his best units at Kharkov, hoping to bleed Vatutin dry.

With victory in sight, Vatutin got a bit overconfident and ordered a series of costly frontal assaults that allowed the Germans to inflict near-crippling losses on the 5th Guards Tank Army. Nevertheless, Manstein ordered Kempf to evacuate Kharkov – against Hitler's orders – before he was surrounded, and the city fell on 22 August. The victory cost Vatutin over 156,000 casualties and 1,864 tanks, but Operation *Rumantsyev* had achieved its objectives and set the stage for a rapid advance to the Dnepr River. The day after Kharkov fell, AOK 6 began to retreat from the Mius River under heavy pressure and Kempf was relieved by Hitler for losing Kharkov. Armeeabteilung Kempf was renamed AOK 8 and placed under General der Infanterie Otto Wöhler. On 27 August, Hitler flew out to Vinnitsa to meet with Manstein to discuss the latest defeats. Manstein pressed Hitler to adopt a policy of 'flexible defence' that allowed tactical withdrawals in order to mass forces for counterattacks as during the 'backhand blow', but Hitler forbade any more retreats. Manstein also urged Hitler to evacuate AOK 17 from the Kuban in order to release some of its 21 divisions to reinforce Heeresgruppe Süd, but Hitler refused this as well.

Manstein meets with Generalmajor Hans Speidel, chief of staff of AOK 8, during the retreat to the Dnepr River in September 1943. Speidel was closely involved with the conspiracy against Hitler but managed to survive. (Bundesarchiv, Bild 101I-705-0262-06, Fotograf: Mahla)

By the end of August, Manstein was facing defeat on virtually all fronts. Heeresgruppe Süd suffered 133,000 casualties in August but received only 33,000 replacements. The five Soviet fronts attacking Heeresgruppe Süd had also suffered heavy losses, but they still had over 2.6 million men and 2,400 tanks against Manstein's 800,000 men and 500 tanks. Manstein played for time, using small counterattacks to bruise the Soviet armoured spearheads, but after the loss of Kharkov he knew that the only hope for halting the powerful Soviet offensives was to establish a new defensive line on the Dnepr River. On 8 September, Hitler flew to Zaporozhe to meet again with Manstein, who pleaded for permission to withdraw behind the Dnepr, but Hitler refused. Hitler did authorize the evacuation of the Kuban but stipulated that AOK 17 would defend the Crimea, not reinforce Manstein's forces. It was not until 15 September – with Heeresgruppe Süd's defences crumbling virtually everywhere – that Hitler authorized Manstein to retreat behind the Dnepr. However, Hitler decided to transfer Hollidt's AOK 6 to Kleist's Heeresgruppe A, leaving Manstein with only three armies to defend the Dnepr line between Kiev and Dnepropetrovsk.

It all became academic a few days later, when the Stavka released Rybalko's rebuilt 3rd Guards Tank Army to Vatutin. Rybalko was assigned the sole mission of punching through the remaining flotsam from 4. Panzerarmee in his path and establishing a bridgehead across the Dnepr. In an amazing display of operational mobility, Rybalko advanced 160km (100 miles) in two days and actually made it to the Dnepr before most of the retreating German units. Rybalko then established a bridgehead over the Dnepr at Bukrin on 22 September and the 5th Guards Tank Army secured another bridgehead at Kremenchug on 29 September. Manstein had confidently expected to gain a reprieve once his exhausted troops were securely positioned behind the Dnepr but he was now shocked to find out that the Soviets had already punctured the formidable barrier before his main forces had even reached safety. Instead of a reprieve, Manstein was now forced to fight a desperate battle to eliminate the Soviet bridgeheads before they could be expanded.

The loss of Kiev

By late September 1943, Manstein's forces were arrayed with Hoth's 4. Panzerarmee defending the Kiev area, Wöhler's AOK 8 holding the area between Cherkassy and Kremenchug and Mackensen's 1. Panzerarmee holding the area around Dnepropetrovsk. Although these forces had taken a severe beating in the retreat to the Dnepr, some of the Panzer units were still formidable and Manstein tried to use them to eliminate the Soviet bridgeheads. Hoth used XLVIII Panzerkorps to mount a strong counterattack that nearly wiped out the Bukrin bridgehead on 27 September and XIII AK to attack the 38th Army's bridgehead at Lyutezh north of Kiev. After the withdrawal behind the Dnepr, Manstein's headquarters was initially in Kirovograd, but he then moved back to Vinnitsa.

In October, the Stavka developed a new plan to exploit the bridgeheads over the Dnepr and encircle Wöhler's AOK 8, which was considered to be the weak link in Manstein's front. While Malinovsky's Southwest Front attacked Dnepropetrovsk to fix the 1. Panzerarmee, Konev's Steppe Front would break out of the Kremenchug bridgehead on Wöhler's right flank, while Vatutin's Voronezh Front (later renamed 1st Ukrainian Front) broke out of the Bukrin bridgehead with Rybalko's 3rd Guards Tank Army. Konev's front scored a major success at Kremenchug, smashing LVII Panzerkorps and then advancing nearly 70km (44 miles) with the 5th Guards Tank Army to the outskirts of Manstein's headquarters at Kirovograd. Malinovsky also enjoyed some success against 1. Panzerarmee, capturing Dnepropetrovsk and Zaporozhe. However, Vatutin's efforts to break out of the Bukrin bridgehead were frustrated by XLVIII Panzerkorps, which fought Rybalko's tankers to a standstill. The Soviet offensive succeeded in pushing most of Wöhler's army back from the Dnepr, except for two corps holding the front between Kanev and Cherkassy.

Soviet troops from the Steppe Front attack the retreating 4. Panzerarmee near Poltava on 23 September 1943. A Marder III tank destroyer burns on the right. (RIA Novosti, 67381)

At this point, Vatutin demonstrated a great deal of flexibility as well as a firm understanding of his opponent. While leaving some forces to continue the fight at the Bukrin bridgehead, he quietly moved the 38th and 60th Armies and Rybalko's armour 150km (93 miles) northwards to the Lyutezh bridgehead. On 1 November, Vatutin began strong diversionary attacks at Bukrin. Manstein discounted reports of Soviet armour moving to Lyutezh since he regarded the swampy area as unsuitable for mechanized operations – the same mistake the French had made about the Ardennes Forest in 1940. At dawn on 3 November, Vatutin unleashed a massive artillery preparation against VII and XIII AK ringing the Lyutezh bridgehead. Manstein and Hoth were completely surprised by this attack and before they could effectively respond, Rybalko's 3rd Guards Tank Army struck the crumbling German line and routed three infantry divisions. Vatutin's forces rapidly pushed southwards to Kiev and with virtually no intact combat units left in the area, Hoth was compelled to retreat. Manstein hurriedly shifted XLVIII Panzerkorps from Bukrin but it was too late and Vatutin's troops captured Kiev on 6 November. Maintaining the pressure, Vatutin pushed his forces westwards in pursuit, overrunning Hoth's flimsy rearguards and capturing Zhitomir on 12 November.

Manstein was humiliated that he had been fooled by Vatutin and had lost Kiev so easily. Hitler was furious and relieved Hoth, replacing him with General der Panzertruppe Erhard Raus. The OKH immediately sent Manstein substantial armoured reinforcements to retake Kiev. By 15 November, he had assembled six Panzer divisions in XXIV and XLVIII Panzerkorps south-west of Kiev, with an impressive 585 tanks. Manstein intended to repeat the 'backhand blow', by slashing into the flank of Rybalko's 3rd Guards Tank Army and then recapturing Kiev. Manstein's counterattack succeeded in retaking Zhitomir and inflicted about 30 per cent losses upon Rybalko's army, but it was frustrated by poor weather and terrain conditions. Unlike earlier counteroffensives, Luftwaffe support was minimal. By 25 November, Manstein suspended the counteroffensive since it failed to encircle any Soviet units.

Despite the punishment he had received at the hands of Vatutin since August, Manstein could learn from his opponent. He was particularly impressed by the Soviet artillery divisions, which had been used to smash his defensive lines and he decided to form the 18. Artillerie-Division from existing assets. Once assembled, the division had 116 heavy calibre artillery pieces. On 6 December, XLVIII Panzerkorps, supported by the 18. Artillerie-Division, attacked the 60th Army at Radomyshl. The attack succeeded in isolating some Soviet rifle divisions and inflicting heavy losses, but the German forces lacked the strength to destroy these formations. Continuing the attack, XLVIII Panzerkorps unexpectedly bumped into three Soviet tank corps near Meleni and became involved in a protracted tank battle that inflicted heavy losses on both sides. By 23 December, Manstein was forced to call off the counteroffensive, having failed to recapture Kiev or destroy Rybalko's armour, but he believed that the counteroffensive had crippled the 1st Ukrainian Front and ruined its ability to launch any major offensive operations for some time. Once again, Manstein underestimated his opponents and his evaluation of the situation was incorrect.

Unknown to Manstein, the Stavka reinforced Vatutin's 1st Ukrainian Front to a total of 924,000 men and they struck the front of 4. Panzerarmee on the morning of 24 December with a massive offensive. Vatutin attacked with seven armies up front, totally overwhelming Raus' badly outnumbered forces. Despite desperate counterattacks by XLVIII Panzerkorps, the Soviet 1st Tank Army and 3rd Guards Tank Army rapidly pressed eastwards – demonstrating that Manstein's counteroffensive had not crippled them. On 31 December, Rybalko's armour recaptured Zhitomir. Once again, Manstein's left flank was broken and hanging in the air, with masses of Soviet armour pouring into the gap – the year was ending much as it had begun.

The Korsun Pocket

Manstein realized that the only way to shore up his broken left flank was to take forces from Hube's 1. Panzerarmee on his right flank, as he had done previously in the Donbas. However, Hitler realized that a wholesale transfer of 1. Panzerarmee would jeopardize the Nikopol bridgehead, which he was adamantly against evacuating. Nevertheless, Manstein began to quietly shift parts of Hube's army on 1 January 1944. By this risky transfer, Manstein hoped to free up enough troops to stabilize his left flank but he did so by concealing the scale of this transfer from the OKH and the fact that he was voluntarily giving up territory on the Dnepr bend. The transfer also forced the hard-pressed AOK 6 to take over the front that had been held by 1. Panzerarmee. Emboldened by the departure of Hube's army, Konev launched a major offensive on 5 January that pushed AOK 8 back 40km (25 miles) and captured Kirovograd on 8 January. The transfer of Hube's army temporarily enabled Heeresgruppe Süd to slow down Vatutin's offensive, but once Katukov's 1st Tank Army got within 65km (40 miles) of Manstein's headquarters in Vinnitsa, he evacuated to Proskurov on 5 January. Katukov then shifted direction and drove due south towards Uman, driving a wedge between1. Panzerarmee and AOK 8.

Of course, the wholesale transfer of 1. Panzerarmee and the abandonment of territory on the Dnepr bend did not escape Hitler's notice and he demanded that Manstein report to him personally at Rastenberg on 4 January 1944. Hitler was angered that Manstein had ignored his specific orders not to withdraw from the Dnepr bend and was more concerned with threats to his own authority than Manstein's military arguments. Manstein only made the tense interview worse by bringing up the idea of appointing a commander-in-chief for the entire Eastern Front. Hitler knew that Manstein considered himself as the best candidate for the position and regarded this suggestion as a personal attack on his own authority. Hitler abruptly cut Manstein off and it was clear that their relationship was deteriorating.

Once he returned to Proskurov, Manstein planned Operation *Watutin*, a joint counterattack by 1. Panzerarmee and AOK 8 to cut off and destroy Katukov's 1st Tank Army. However, even if he could stop Katukov's drive on Uman, the boundary between Hube's army and Wöhler's AOK 8 would still be vulnerable in the Korsun salient. The last German foothold on the Dnepr was held by XLII AK, belonging to 1. Panzerarmee, and XI AK, belonging to AOK 8. Even though Manstein requested to withdraw from the Korsun salient before the Soviets cut it off, Hitler forbade Manstein from abandoning the last position on the Dnepr. Already, the Stavka had its eyes on Korsun and Zhukov arrived in mid-January 1944 to coordinate a pincer attack by Vatutin's 1st Ukrainian Front and Konev's 2nd Ukrainian Front in the hope of creating another successful pocket like Stalingrad.

Manstein realized that the Soviets would encircle the Korsun salient and since he was forbidden from evacuating this position, his only two remaining choices were to either deploy his remaining mobile reserves near the salient or to conduct a spoiling attack. In fact, he decided to do both. While Manstein hoped that Operation *Watutin* would delay Vatutin's attack, he ordered Wöhler to keep two Panzer divisions ready to counterattack any Soviet penetration on the eastern side of the salient by Konev's forces. As further insurance, Manstein formed a special mobile fire brigade, known as schwere-Panzer-Regiment 'Bäke', which he could use to deal with any Soviet breakthroughs. This ad hoc unit had a battalion each of Panther and Tiger tanks, plus artillery, engineers and infantry – making it the most powerful formation left in Heeresgruppe Süd.

Operation *Watutin* began on 24 January, but before the counteroffensive could make any progress, Konev

Soviet poster from late 1943: 'The enemy will not escape our revenge!' After Kursk, the Soviets never let up the pressure on Manstein's Heeresgruppe Süd, driving it back until it began to disintegrate. (RIA Novosti, 136592)

Relief of the Korsun Pocket, February 1944

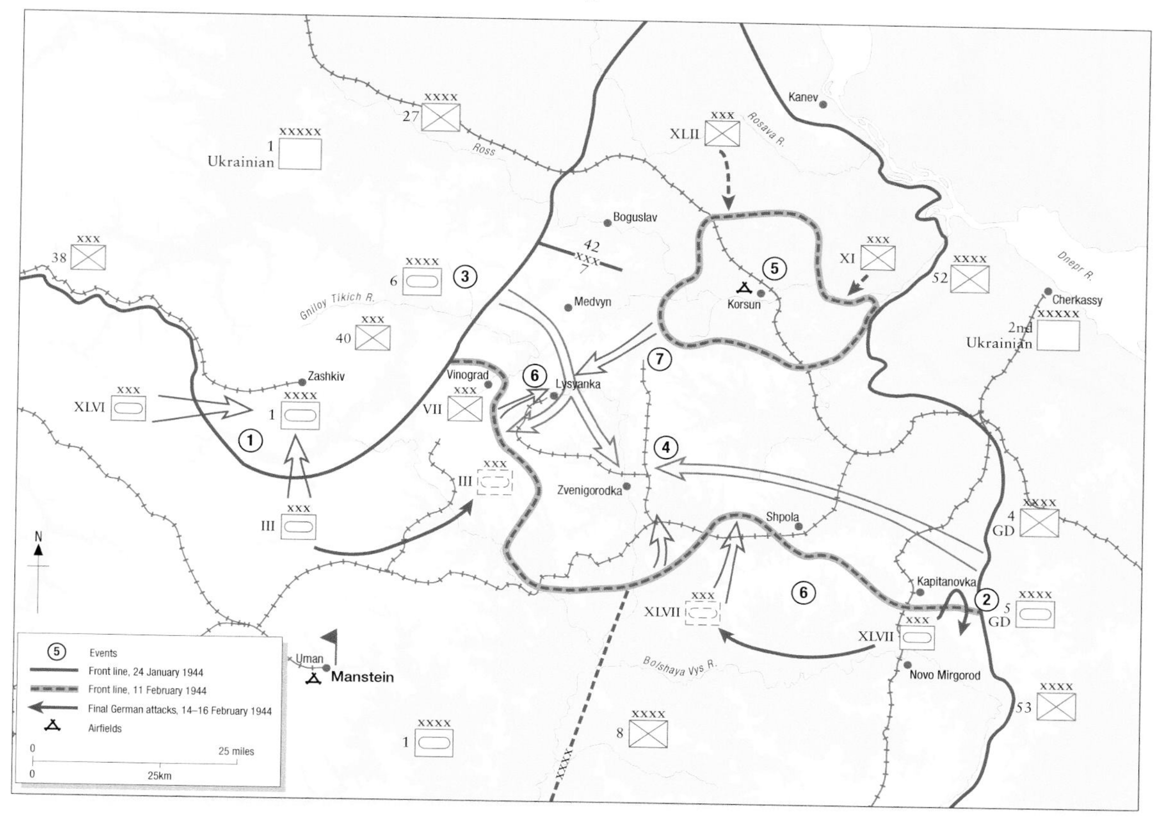

1. 24 January 1944: Manstein begins Operation *Vatutin* to encircle and destroy the Soviet 1st Tank Army before it reaches his headquarters at Uman.
2. 25 January 1944: Konev attacks east side of the Korsun Salient with the 4th Guards Army and 5th Guards Tank Army. Counterattacks by XLVII Panzerkorps fail to stop him from achieving a breakthrough.
3. 26 January 1944: Vatutin attacks the western side of the Korsun Salient with the 40th Army and 6th Tank Army. Although the German VII AK repulses the main attack, Soviet armour exploits a gap between VII and XLII AK.
4. 28 January 1944: the 5th Guards Tank Army and the 6th Tank Army linked up at Zvenigorodka, trapping XI and XLII AK in the Korsun Pocket.
5. 1–10 February 1944: the German forces inside the pocket withdraw inwards to hold a hedgehog defence around the airfield. The two corps are formed into Gruppe Stemmermann.
6. 1 February 1944: Operation *Wanda*, the relief effort, begins with attacks by III and XLVII Panzerkorps to reach the pocket. Although the Germans succeed in advancing 35–40km (22–31 miles) during the next week and III Panzerkorps reaches Lysanka, Vatutin and Konev rush reinforcements to the area and block any further advance.
7. Night, 16–17 February 1944: Gruppe Stemmermann conducts an amazing night breakout operation that succeeds in crossing the last 7km (4 miles) to III Panzerkorps' lines. About two-thirds of the trapped German troops escape, after abandoning their vehicles and heavy equipment.

and Vatutin started their own probing attacks against the Korsun salient. The next morning, Konev concentrated seven rifle divisions, 323 tanks and a great deal of artillery against the German 389. Infanterie-Division, defending a 21km-long (13-mile) stretch of front on the eastern corner of the salient. After the division disintegrated, Konev pushed the 5th Guards Tank Army through to exploit eastwards. Wöhler's Panzer reserves counterattacked but failed to stop the Soviet breakthrough. On the western side of the salient, Vatutin attacked on 26 January with five rifle divisions,

A German truck convoy negotiates a muddy Ukrainian road with difficulty. Manstein's concepts of *Bewegungskrieg* were premised upon an idealized battlefield but rapid manoeuvre often proved difficult in the harsh weather and terrain conditions experienced in the Soviet Union. (Author's collection)

but Hube's well-prepared VII AK failed to break. Then, in a display of operational flexibility characteristic of the heyday of blitzkrieg, Vatutin redirected a mobile group into a gap created by a supporting attack and once these tanks succeeded in getting into the German rear areas, he pushed the 6th Tank Army behind them. On 28 January, the 5th Guards Tank Army and the 6th Tank Army linked up at Zvenigorodka, trapping 56,000 German troops from the XI and XLII AK inside the *Kessel.*

Manstein initiated a Luftwaffe airlift that brought in enough supplies to prevent an immediate collapse by the trapped troops. He was determined not to repeat the mistakes of Stalingrad and he rapidly organized a relief operation by transferring III Panzerkorps and schwere-Panzer-Regiment 'Bäke' as soon as it concluded its role in Operation *Watutin.* He also directed XLVII Panzerkorps to organize a relief attack with its three Panzer divisions. Fortunately, Zhukov directed Konev and Vatutin to concentrate their efforts upon reducing the *Kessel,* which allowed Manstein to construct a screening force across the gap between 1. Panzerarmee and AOK 8. Inside the pocket, the trapped troops were formed into Gruppe Stemmermann and they retreated to a more defensible perimeter, which succeeded in holding an area around the Korsun airfield for the next two weeks.

Operation *Wanda,* the German relief effort, began on 1 February when XLVII Panzerkorps, which had 40 tanks, attacked northwards against Konev's forces. The distance between the *Kessel* and the relief forces was 35–40km (22–25 miles), but extremely muddy conditions seriously reduced German mobility. On 3 February, the stronger III Panzerkorps, with 164 tanks, began its own attack against Vatutin's forces. Soviet resistance was fierce, since Konev and Vatutin had positioned six rifle, three tank and one mechanized corps between the relief force and the *Kessel.* After a week of attacking, neither German corps had advanced more than 20–25km (12–16 miles). Manstein and his staff moved up to Uman in his command train to supervise the operation and ensure the closest coordination between Hube and Wöhler.

Throughout the relief operation, Manstein argued with Hitler about the necessity of Gruppe Stemmermann conducting a breakout once the relief forces approached. Once again, Hitler clung to the idea that Korsun could be held once a link-up occurred. Manstein knew that Gruppe Stemmermann was running out of time and he ordered III Panzerkorps, reinforced with the 1. SS-Panzer-Division 'Leibstandarte SS Adolf Hitler', to make another push on 11 February. III Panzerkorps succeeded in advancing 15km (9 miles) and reached Lysanka, within 7km (4 miles) of the trapped forces in the *Kessel,* but Zhukov positioned several tank corps that blocked any further advance. On the same day, Gruppe Stemmermann lost control of Korsun airfield. Even though Hitler had not approved a breakout, Manstein directly radioed Stemmermann on 16 February and ordered him to conduct a breakout that evening. The Germans inside the pocket skilfully organized a night exfiltration and they managed to achieve sufficient tactical surprise for the bulk of the combat troops to penetrate the Soviet cordon and reach III Panzerkorps at Lysanka, at the cost of abandoning their vehicles and artillery. However, once the breakout was detected, the Soviets unleashed their cavalry and artillery against the German support troops, most of whom were massacred or captured. All told, 40,423 Germans escaped the *Kessel*, but 19,000 were killed or captured.

Although Manstein succeeded in rescuing over 40,000 of the troops trapped inside the Korsun Pocket, XI and XLII AK lost virtually all of their equipment. (RIA Novosti, 187)

While the breakout from the Korsun pocket reduced the scale of the Soviet victory, the fact remained that all six divisions that escaped were ruined. Indeed, 5. SS-Panzer-Division 'Wiking' was the only division that was ever rebuilt. Furthermore, the relief forces had suffered over 4,000 casualties themselves and lost about 240 tanks and assault guns. Manstein's designated fire brigade, schwere-Panzer-Regiment 'Bäke', claimed to have destroyed about 400 Soviet tanks in its month-long existence but it had so few tanks operational by late February that it was disbanded. Although Manstein's rescue effort saved lives in the short run, it had essentially consumed the last mobile reserves available to Heeresgruppe Süd.

Hube's Pocket

After the end of the Korsun operation, Manstein expected Vatutin to continue his offensive against the weak left flank of Heeresgruppe Süd, while Konev pounded away at AOK 8. In fact, Zhukov switched the main effort to strike the boundary of Raus' 4. Panzerarmee and Hube's 1. Panzerarmee near Tarnopol, while Konev hit Hube's right flank. Once Hube's flanks were penetrated, Vatutin and Konev each had three tank armies to conduct deep mobile operations to encircle the entire 1. Panzerarmee. The Stavka was determined to destroy Heeresgruppe Süd and it took the unprecedented step of massing all six of its tank armies against just one of Manstein's armies. However, five days before the offensive was to start, Ukrainian partisans fatally wounded Vatutin. Zhukov stepped in and took direct command over the 1st Ukrainian Front.

Even if Manstein had known Zhukov's intent, there was little that he could do to stop it, given the dilapidated condition of Heeresgruppe Süd. At the beginning of March, Heeresgruppe Süd was holding an 843km-wide (524-mile) front with only 37 and a half understrength divisions and its armour reserves exhausted after the Korsun relief effort. Zhukov's 1st Ukrainian began the offensive on 4 March and Konev's Front joined the next day. Despite fierce German resistance, breakthroughs were achieved, enabling Zhukov and Konev to commit their tank armies. Hube's army had both flanks enveloped by Soviet armour, leaving 1. Panzerarmee in a salient around the town of Kamenets-Podolsky. Manstein was forced to evacuate his headquarters again, this time back to Lwów. By mid-March, the Soviet pincers had nearly encircled 1. Panzerarmee, but Hitler refused Manstein's requests to evacuate the salient. On 28 March, the trap shut when 6th Tank Army captured Khotin, closing off Hube's escape route.

Virtually the entire 1. Panzerarmee with about 200,000 men and 20 divisions were trapped inside the *Kessel*. This time, Manstein had nothing left to mount a relief operation and could only re-establish a thin front across the Carpathians by using the Hungarian 1st Army. Flying to Berlin, he pointed out to Hitler that his favourite 1. SS-Panzer-Division 'Leibstandarte SS Adolf Hitler' and 2. SS-Panzer-Division 'Das Reich' were both trapped inside the *Kessel* and would be lost unless reinforcements arrived to mount a rescue effort. Hitler reluctantly agreed to provide SS-Obergruppenführer Willi Bittrich's II SS-Panzerkorps from the west to mount a rescue operation, but he was adamant that Hube's trapped forces remain in place until the rescue force reopened their supply lines. Manstein agreed but he knew that the Luftwaffe could not sustain this large a force by air. As soon as he returned to his headquarters, Manstein disregarded Hitler's orders and instructed Hube to begin moving the *Kessel* westwards to link up with the 4. Panzerarmee and the expected relief force. Hube disagreed with Manstein because the distance to German lines in the west was about 100km (62 miles), whereas the distance to the Romanian IV Army in the south was half that, even though this would make it more difficult to establish a new front line. Once again, Manstein had to work with a headstrong subordinate who regarded his orders merely as suggestions.

However, Zhukov made two critical mistakes when he encircled the 1. Panzerarmee: he expected the trapped forces to make a breakout to the south and he did not reckon with the tenacity and resourcefulness of Generaloberst Hans-Valentin Hube. Instead of just sitting tight and waiting for relief as Paulus had, Hube attacked the relatively weakly held western flank of the *Kessel* and began to push outwards. Hube reorganized his forces and managed to keep enough troops and tanks operational to keep moving – which surprised Zhukov because up to that point, trapped German units had generally remained static to hold airfields for resupply. Yet since the Luftwaffe could not supply Hube's army, there was no point in staying in place. When the breakout effort began on 27 March, it appeared to be going well, but Manstein would not see it through to its conclusion. Hitler realized that Hube was in fact giving up territory rather than waiting for rescue and decided that Manstein had defied his orders once too often.

On 30 March, Manstein was ordered to report to Hitler at the Obersalzberg, where he was informed that Walther Model was replacing him. Hitler softened the relief by awarding Manstein the Swords to his Ritterkreuz and told him that, 'the time for grand-style operations in the east, for which I had been particularly qualified, was now past. All that counted now was to cling stubbornly to what we held.' Hitler also said that he regarded Manstein as one of his 'most capable commanders' and that he would give him another assignment in the near future. As a postscript to Manstein's last operational decisions, Hube's troops managed to fight their way through Soviet lines and linked up with Bittrich's relief force on 6 April, thereby depriving Zhukov of his triumph.

OPPOSING COMMANDERS

Manstein fought against a number of Soviet commanders, but his most inveterate opponent was Nikolai Vatutin. Despite coming from a peasant background and being 14 years younger than Manstein, Vatutin proved to be just as capable of conducting manoeuvre warfare. Indeed, Vatutin proved to be Manstein's nemesis, defeating him at Soltsy in August 1941 and then hounding him across the Ukraine in 1943, then snatching Kiev from his grasp with a brilliant manoeuvre. Manstein only defeated Vatutin once – in February 1943 – and Vatutin learned from this experience and never allowed his spearheads to be destroyed piecemeal again.

Like Manstein, Vatutin had been a General Staff officer before the war and he was actively involved in mobilization and war plans in the late 1930s. However, Vatutin did not shun politics but instead joined the Communist Party and he was well regarded by Stalin and Zhukov. Vatutin played a key role in delaying the German drive on Leningrad, then encircling the first large German pocket at Demyansk. Shifted southwards in July 1942, Vatutin's Southwest Front later frustrated Manstein's relief of the Stalingrad *Kessel* and then came close to encircling Heeresgruppe Don itself. Vatutin's only serious misjudgement against Manstein occurred in February 1943, when he failed to detect the impending German counteroffensive until his over-extended forces were being cut to ribbons. Unlike Manstein, Vatutin learned from this defeat and took the measure of his opponent.

At Kursk, Vatutin was able to stop Manstein's powerful armoured spearheads well short of their objectives and then shift to a counteroffensive that shattered the German front. Vatutin surprised Manstein at Belgorod in August and thoroughly outmanoeuvred him at Kiev in December. Vatutin demonstrated great flexibility during the Korsun offensive, taking advantage of fleeting opportunities rather than reinforcing failure, which resulted in his armour encircling two German corps. However, Vatutin was unable to prevent Manstein from relieving the Korsun Pocket, but this limited success squandered Manstein's last operational reserves. Vatutin would surely have played a major role in finishing off Manstein's command in the Kamenets-Podolsky offensive if Ukrainian partisans had not fatally wounded him after Korsun. Nevertheless, Vatutin had demonstrated that Manstein's style of *Bewegungskrieg* did not work against a steady opponent and that the Red Army had some commanders who could turn the tables and conduct a form of manoeuvre warfare that astonished even Manstein.

General Nikolai Vatutin, commander of the Voronezh Front in early July 1943. (RIA Novosti, 3900)

WHEN WAR IS DONE

After he was relieved of command, Manstein went back to his family in Dresden and was assigned to the Führer Reserve. As the situation grew worse on all fronts, he confidently expected to be recalled to duty but no orders ever came. Hitler was convinced that Manstein was not capable of obeying his stand-fast orders and conducting a fanatical defence, which made him poorly suited to the situation facing Germany by mid-1944. Circumstances had forced the Wehrmacht to abandon *Bewegungskrieg* in favour of *Stellungskrieg*.

While sitting on his hands in Dresden, Manstein was aware of the conspiracy within the army to eliminate Hitler. He had been approached three times by representatives of the conspiracy in 1943, including a meeting with Major Claus von Stauffenberg. Each time, Manstein listened to the arguments against Hitler's interference with military operations, but refused to commit to any action against the regime. Manstein simply replied that, 'Prussian field marshals do not mutiny' and steadfastly stuck to his loyalty oath to Hitler. Two of his senior staff officers at Heeresgruppe Süd – Oberst Eberhard Finckh and Oberstleutnant Schulze-Büttger – were involved in the conspiracy and were executed after the failed attempt on Hitler's life on 20 July 1944. Manstein knew that the conspirators intended to kill Hitler but he said nothing, leaving the door open to either cooperate with a new regime if a coup succeeded or to deny involvement if it failed. Although neither Göring nor Himmler trusted Manstein, he did not come under serious suspicion after the conspiracy failed.

By late January 1945, Konev's 1st Ukrainian Front was nearly on Manstein's doorstep and he decided to flee westwards with his family. He still had sufficient influence to secure two army trucks to load his personal belongings and together with his wife, son Rüdiger and his adjutant, they headed west to Hamburg. On the way, Manstein stopped in Berlin, but Hitler refused to see him. Continuing on to Hamburg, Manstein sought out Generalfeldmarschall Fedor von Bock, who had also been relieved by Hitler. Together, they went to see Großadmiral Karl Dönitz, who became the new head of state after Hitler's suicide. Manstein expected that Dönitz would choose him as the new commander-in-chief of the army, but instead Dönitz picked Generalfeldmarschall Ferdinand Schörner. Crestfallen, Manstein left Dönitz's headquarters empty-handed. After sending his adjutant to make contact with the advancing British forces, Manstein surrendered to Field Marshal Montgomery at the elegant Hotel Atlantic in Hamburg on 5 May 1945. On 26 August, he was taken to England as a prisoner of war.

Manstein passed his first year in captivity quietly, but in August 1946 he was brought to Nuremberg to be part of a special defence team, which included Halder and Rundstedt, for the 'OKW Trial'. During the trial, Manstein tried to conceal the collusion between the army and the Nazi regime and argued that the SS were solely responsible for any war crimes. Manstein was cross-examined by the American prosecutor Telford Taylor, who inconveniently produced a copy of his 20 November 1941 order, which said that, 'the Jewish-Bolshevist system has to be exterminated for all times' and encouraged his troops to treat the local population harshly. Taylor ruthlessly ripped apart Manstein's flimsy excuses and exposed him as a liar. As a witness for the defence, Manstein was a failure and he failed to prevent his former comrades – Leeb, Hoth, Reinhardt, Hollidt and Wöhler – from all being found guilty of war crimes and receiving prison terms. In particular, Wöhler was convicted for his role in working with Einsatzgruppe D 'special actions' during his time as chief of staff of AOK 11 in the Crimea.

German troops burn Ukrainian villages as they retreat westwards in early 1944. Manstein's use of 'scorched earth' tactics resulted in his conviction for war crimes in 1949. (Nik Cornish, WH 738)

After Manstein's involvement in Nazi atrocities in the Soviet Union became public, he soon found himself before a British military tribunal, with charges that focused on allegations of mistreatment of prisoners of war and civilians in the Soviet Union, as well as use of scorched earth tactics. When the trial began in Hamburg in August 1949, Manstein was confident that he could gain an acquittal by denying any knowledge of war crimes committed in his areas of operation, but this proved to be a major mistake once the prosecution produced documents revealing his condoning the use of terrorism against the civil population. Even worse, the former commander of Einsatzgruppe D testified that he had coordinated 'special actions' with the AOK 11 staff. Manstein proved to be very poor at defending himself in court, particularly in regard to charges that he had ordered the execution of Soviet political officers during the advance on Leningrad. Incredibly, Manstein argued that commissars – who wore military uniforms in compliance with the Hague Convention – were not protected by international law. Despite attracting sympathy during his trial, even from former opponents such as Winston Churchill and Montgomery, Manstein was found guilty on two of the 17 charges and sentenced to 18 years in prison.

Manstein spent the next four years in prison, but he was released for 'good behaviour' in May 1953. Afterwards, he returned to his family and wrote his memoirs, *Verlorene Siege* (*Lost Victories*), in 1955 and then *Aus Einem Soldatenleben* (*From a Soldier's Life*) in 1958. When West Germany began establishing the Bundeswehr, Manstein and a number of retired senior Wehrmacht officers were brought in to advise upon the formation of the new army. For a brief moment, between November 1955 and June 1956, Manstein was back to writing memorandums about military organization and some of his recommendations on brigade structure were used. However, the West German Government was reticent to allow a convicted war criminal too prominent a place in the Bundeswehr and he was gradually sidelined once the new army got on its feet. By the early 1960s, Manstein's ideas on manoeuvre warfare were increasingly irrelevant to a Bundeswehr that was oriented strictly toward defence. Since his former home was now in East Germany, he moved his family to the village of Irschenhausen, south of Munich. He became involved in veterans' affairs and writing. His wife Jutta died in March 1966, leaving him alone and in failing health. On 10 June 1973, von Manstein died of a stroke at the age of 85.

INSIDE THE MIND

Manstein always tried to portray himself as a cerebral chess-player, who cunningly waited for his opponent to make a mistake and then at the right moment, delivered a lethal strike at a critical point by means of an unexpected manoeuvre. In terms of the principles of war, Manstein's operational style put greatest emphasis on surprise, manoeuvre and offensive – which were the hallmarks of the doctrine developed by Hans von Seeckt for the Reichswehr back in 1921. In *Sichelschnitt*, *Trappenjagd* and the 'backhand blow', Manstein sought to defeat stronger opponents by means of a surprise attack from an unexpected quarter and each succeeded. However, *Bewegungskrieg* was an integral part of German war making after the costly experience with *Stellungskrieg* in World War I, though not all German commanders were as ardent an advocate of manoeuvre warfare as Manstein.

Manstein's operational plans also paid great heed to the principles of simplicity and mass, by carefully weighting his main *Schwerpunkt* with combat modifiers (engineers, assault guns) and then employing the bare minimum of independent formations. Rather than constantly trying to seek a classic Cannae-style double envelopment, Manstein preferred simple single envelopments, which worked in the Ardennes and the Kerch Peninsula. He also had an excellent grasp of time and space considerations, which is a vital prerequisite for effective battlefield command. Probably the only principle of war that Manstein failed to employ properly was economy of force. Limited resources forced Manstein to accept great risk in some sectors in order to mass his best forces for offensive action, but this required a good assessment of enemy intentions and capabilities – which was not Manstein's strong suit. Time and again, Manstein miscalculated Soviet intentions and left small German blocking forces exposed to encirclement, as occurred with Sponeck's troops at Kerch in December 1941 and Armeeabteilung Hollidt during *Zitadelle*.

Manstein's son Rüdiger later said that his father's greatest weakness was his inability to understand that he could not persuade Hitler with pure military logic. It is clear that Manstein's relationship with Hitler was only good when he produced victories, but Hitler never really trusted him. Although Manstein complained about Hitler's interference, he actually had a relatively free hand as AOK 11 commander in the Crimea. It was not until

Manstein took over Heeresgruppe Don that he found his concept of *Bewegungskrieg* hamstrung by Hitler's obsession with holding first the Kuban, then Rostov, then the Donbas region, then Kharkov. Forced to hold specific territorial objectives at all costs, Manstein was obliged to fight a *Stellungskrieg* in some sectors of his front, thereby reducing the forces available for counterattacks. However, Manstein's style was ill suited to prevailing circumstances once Germany lost the initiative after Kursk and his methods were essentially reduced to trading space for time and preventing his armies from being encircled. As a defensive commander, Manstein was far less successful than Kesselring, Model or Raus in containing enemy offensives.

As a commander, Manstein's interaction with subordinates was often problematic. He was rarely willing to stick his neck out making tough command decisions that could endanger his position and he failed to support his subordinates (Sponeck, Hausser, Lanz, Kempf, Hoth) when they took actions to save their commands. Indeed, Manstein showed little loyalty to his subordinates throughout the war and seemed to regard himself as irreplaceable on the Eastern Front. As a leader, Manstein lacked the charisma or dominant personality to impose his will on headstrong subordinates such as Hoth, Hausser and Hube, who often ignored his directives. Indeed, Manstein had an effete side to his character that was demonstrated in his preference for luxuries such as his command train, headquartering in castles far from the front and his nightly bridge games. His front-line commanders respected his operational skill but his lack of 'guts' did not inspire others. Dietrich von Choltitz, who commanded a regiment at Sevastopol, later commented that Hitler didn't respect Manstein much either and would 'dig [him] in the paunch with his elbow' at meetings.[2]

Manstein at Nuremberg in 1946. His knowledge of *Einsatzgruppen* activities in the Crimea was exposed during the hearings and he was eventually convicted on two charges of war crimes and served four additional years in captivity. (Author's collection)

Politically, Manstein's views were simplistic in the extreme – like those of many career officers – and he initially resented the Nazi regime. However, once his anti-Hitler superiors fell like ninepins and his own career was threatened, Manstein had a change of heart. When Hitler adopted his *Sichelschnitt* recommendations, Manstein became a devoted follower and admired the Führer until late 1942. Although Manstein found the *Kommissar Befehl* of 1941 distasteful, he obeyed it. In the Crimea, Manstein decided to toe the Nazi line adopted by his superior Reichenau and issued his own order authorizing his troops to 'exterminate the Judeo-Bolshevist' system. He almost certainly held racist views against Jews and Slavs prior to the war, based upon his attitudes toward Poland and Czechoslovakia. When some of his aides protested about nearby SS 'special actions', he ignored them. Indeed, Manstein's

2. Sönke Neitzel (ed.), *Tapping Hitler's Generals* (Frontline Books: St Paul, 2007)

criticism of Hitler was never about Nazi policies, but about the Führer's interference with his command prerogatives.

Although Manstein rebuffed all efforts to bring him into the anti-Hitler conspiracy, he routinely mocked the Führer openly among his own staff, referring to him in a sarcastic tone as 'the greatest military mind of all time'. This sotto voce opposition was highly unprofessional in eroding military discipline and demonstrated his lack of moral courage. Manstein whined constantly about Hitler's interference but always knuckled under. Guderian noticed this and said that Manstein 'never had a good day' when dealing with Hitler.

A LIFE IN WORDS

Although relatively unknown outside the Wehrmacht until 1940, Manstein emerged to garner immense prestige and recognition in 1941–42. On 10 January 1944, Manstein was on the cover of the American news magazine *Time*. Not flashy like Rommel or tough like Model, Manstein set about developing the image of himself as a brilliant 'chess player', who used his superior mind to overcome his opponents.

Within the Wehrmacht, opinions were divided about Manstein. A great number of senior officers regarded him as arrogant, particularly for the tendency he demonstrated on the Generalstab to ignore the viewpoints of others. His former mentor Ludwig Beck eventually broke off his friendship with Manstein and later said that he was 'not a man of bad character, but a man of no character at all'. Guderian cooperated with Manstein to develop the *Sichelschnitt* plan – which Manstein failed to mention in his memoirs – and felt that Manstein tried to grab all the credit for himself, even though he had no direct knowledge of Panzer operations at the time. Guderian did acknowledge Manstein as 'our finest operational brain', but regarded him more as an ideal staff officer, rather than as a battlefield commander. Later, Wolfram von Richthofen, commander of Fliegerkorps VIII and a close collaborator with Manstein in 1942–43, said that 'he is the best tactician and combat commander we have'.

Manstein's memoirs, *Lost Victories*, appeared in Germany in 1955 and these memoirs were particularly noticeable for the manner in which the author glossed or omitted any items related to the war crimes for which he had just served four years in prison. Instead of focusing on his own wartime activities, the author used *Lost Victories* to build the case that Germany could have won the war in the east – or at least achieved a draw – if Hitler had listened to his generals and allowed them to conduct the kind of manoeuvre warfare at which the Wehrmacht excelled. Thus Manstein laid the blame for the demise of *Bewegungskrieg* squarely on Hitler's doorstep, accusing him of 'throwing victory away'. He also suggested that he was himself uniquely qualified to be made supreme commander of the Eastern Front and Hitler's failure to do so was one of his greatest mistakes. *Lost Victories* was very well received by Western audiences, particularly British military writers such as Basil Liddell Hart, who viewed Manstein's methods as the epitome of the 'indirect approach'. Hart lavished praise on Manstein, writing that, 'the ablest of all the German generals was probably Field Marshall Erich von Manstein. He had a superb strategic sense, combined with a greater understanding of mechanized weapons than any of the generals who did not belong to the tank school itself.'

Due to the success and readability of *Lost Victories* as well as recognition of his role in developing the 1940 *Sichelschnitt* plan, other historians echoed Hart's evaluation and began to speak of Manstein as 'Hitler's most brilliant general' and the 'foremost practitioner of large-scale mechanized warfare'. However, Hitler himself regarded Walther Model as his 'best Generalfeldmarschall', probably followed by Erwin Rommel. Claims that Manstein was a great armoured commander ignore the fact that he never had more than a single Panzer division under his control as either a corps or army commander and that he never commanded a *Panzerarmee*. By the time that he did gain control over a number of Panzer divisions, as an army group commander, he was far removed from their day-to-day activities. Claims that Manstein was a 'superb strategist' also seem untenable, since he never served in the OKW or OKH in wartime.

Indeed, Manstein's reputation is almost entirely based on just three factors: his role in *Sichelschnitt*, the capture of Sevastopol and the 'backhand blow', all of which figure prominently in *Lost Victories*. His defeats, beginning at Soltsy in 1941 and extending to the loss of Kiev, are glossed over in his memoirs and poorly known. Today, he is still regarded by many as an 'operational genius', but Manstein did not attract biography writers after the war, unlike flashier commanders such as Erwin Rommel. Due to Manstein's conviction for war crimes and the anti-Semitism he demonstrated in his trial, he did not appear to be a sympathetic figure for biographers. Today, Manstein's legacy has begun a slide into relative obscurity, as memories of his victories fade and modern Germany has little need for remembering his principles of *Bewegungskrieg*.

FURTHER READING

Glantz, David M., *From the Don to the Dnepr* Frank Cass: London, 1991

Manstein, Erich von, *Soldat im 20. Jahrhundert: Militärisch-politische Nachlese* Bernard & Graefe: Bonn, 5th Edition, 2002

——, *Aus einem Soldatenleben, 1887–1939* Athenaum-Verlag: Bonn, 1958

——, *Lost Victories* Presidio Press: Novato, CA, 1982

Manstein, Erich von, and Franz Kurowski, *An den Brennpunkten des Zweiten Weltkrieges. Werdegang und Kriegseinsatz eines Feldmarschalls* Bublies-Verlag: Schnellbach, 2004

Nipe Jr., George M. *Last Victory in Russia: The SS-Panzerkorps and Manstein's Counteroffensive February–March 1943* Schiffer Military History: Atglen, PA, 2000

Sadarananda, Dana V., *Beyond Stalingrad: Manstein and the Operations of Army Group Don* Praeger Publishers: New York, 1990

Stahlberg, Alexander von, *Die verdammte Pflicht. Erinnerungen 1932 bis 1945* Ullstein TB: Berlin, 9th Edition, 1998

INDEX

Figures in **bold** refer to illustrations

£4-65

ROD ELLIS &
BRIAN TOMLINSON

SPEAKING

INTERMEDIATE

OXFORD SUPPLEMENTARY SKILLS

SERIES EDITOR: ALAN MALEY

OXFORD UNIVERSITY PRESS

Oxford University Press
Walton Street, Oxford OX2 6DP

Oxford New York Toronto Madrid
Delhi Bombay Calcutta Madras Karachi
Kuala Lumpur Singapore Hong Kong Tokyo
Nairobi Dar es Salaam Cape Town
Melbourne Auckland

and associated companies in
Berlin Ibadan

ISBN 0 19 453410 3

First published 1987
Fourth impression 1994

Set by Promenade Graphics Limited, Cheltenham

Printed in Hong Kong

CONTENTS

ACKNOWLEDGEMENTS

We should like to thank the following writers and publishers for permission to use texts which fall within their copyright:

John Arden and Penguin Books Ltd for the poem 'Phineus' from *The Happy Haven*, New English Dramatists 4 (1962); T.E. Johnson and Educational Explorers for an extract from *One Off* in the My Life and My Work Series; Geoffrey Matthews and Heinemann Educational Books for an extract from *The Space Invaders* (Heinemann Guided Readers).

Illustrations by:
Andy Bylo
Jane Cradock-Watson
Penny Dann
Karen Daws
David Langdon
Trevor Mason
David Murray
Punch Publications Ltd
John Ridgway
Susan Scott

The publishers would like to thank the following for their permission to reproduce photographs:
All-Sport
J. Allan Cash
Austin J. Brown
Britannia Airways
Central Independent Television
Format
Sally and Richard Greenhill
London Weekend Television
National Coal Board
National Railway Museum
Network
Science Photo Library
Brian and Sally Shuel
Sporting Pictures
Syndication International
Topham

Location photography by:
Rob Judges
Julian Prentis

The publishers would like to thank the following for their help and assistance:

Chambre de Commerce et d'Industrie de Calais
Sinclair Vehicles Ltd
Swan School of English

FOREWORD

This series covers the four skill areas of Listening, Speaking, Reading and Writing at four levels — elementary, intermediate, upper-intermediate and advanced. Although we have decided to retain the traditional division of language use into the 'four skills', the skills are not treated in total isolation. In any given book the skill being dealt with serves as the *focus* of attention and is always interwoven with and supported by other skills. This enables teachers to concentrate on skills development without losing touch with the more complex reality of language use.

Our authors have had in common the following principles, that material should be:

- creative — both through author-creativity leading to interesting materials, and through their capacity to provoke creative responses from students;
- interesting — both for their cognitive and affective content, and for the activities required of the learners.
- fluency-focused — bringing in accuracy work only in so far as it is necessary to the completion of an activity;
- task-based — rather than engaging in closed exercise activities, to use tasks with pay-offs for the learners;
- problem-solving focused — so as to engage students in cognitive effort and thus provoke meaningful interaction;
- humanistic — in the sense that the materials speak to and interrelate with the learners as real people and engage them in interaction grounded in their own experience;
- learning-centred — by ensuring that the materials promote learning and help students to develop their own strategies for learning. This is in opposition to the view that a pre-determined content is taught and identically internalized by all students. In our materials we do not expect input to equal intake.

By ensuring continuing consultation between and among authors at different levels, and by piloting the materials, the levels have been established on a pragmatic basis. The fact that the authors, between them, share a wide and varied body of experience has made this possible without losing sight of the need to pitch materials and tasks at an attainable level while still allowing for the spice of challenge.

There are three main ways in which these materials can be used:

- as a supplement to a core course book;
- as self-learning material. Most of the books can be used on an individual basis with a minimum of teacher guidance, though the interactive element is thereby lost.
- as modular course material. A teacher might, for instance, combine intermediate *Listening* and *Speaking* books with upper-intermediate *Reading* and elementary *Writing* with a class which had a good passive knowledge of English but which needed a basic grounding in writing skills.

(Alan Maley, Madras 1986)

INTRODUCTION TO THE TEACHER

Aims of this book

This book is designed to help students become more fluent in their use of English. It is based on the principle that talking in English can help learners to both learn new language and also to develop the ability to communicate easily and naturally. It is not a book, therefore, that is intended to practise correct usage. It is expected that the teacher will use this book in conjunction with more formal language teaching materials that concentrate on correct usage.

The first units in the book focus primarily on providing opportunities for using English fluently. The later units continue this focus but also introduce some activities requiring reflection on language form. In all the units, however, the principal aim is to develop fluency.

The materials

This book consists of activities rather than exercises. That is, the materials are designed to open up possibilities for students to express their own opinions and to use their imaginations freely, without worrying unduly about correct usage. No attempt has been made to design activities focused on specific language points.

The book is divided into units. Each unit has a theme (e.g. Sport or Marriage). Each theme is divided into a number of topics (e.g. Sport is divided into Rules, Rise to fame, Crossword and Sporting definitions). For each topic there are a number of activities, nearly all of which are 'open' in the sense that there is no single correct answer. In general the units at the beginning of the book are less linguistically demanding than the later units.

Students are likely to find many of the activities challenging their linguistic, intellectual and imaginative capacities. This is deliberate. We have tried to avoid trivial activities and to involve the students in *what* they are talking about. The activities will have succeeded if the students become interested in getting their ideas across rather than worrying about linguistic form. Different students will be able to operate at different levels when they are doing the same activities. Some will be able to express complex ideas and others only simple ideas and also some will be able to use quite complex language and others only simple language. Sometimes students will be given a choice of activities which are at different levels of difficulty. The teacher should always be prepared to accept different levels of achievement from the students and encourage them to perform to the best of their individual abilities rather than to compete against each other.

Most of the activities in the book are interactive. They have been designed to enable the students to talk with each other in conversation. However, there are also a few activities where the students are required to give short presentations on topics that have been prepared previously. Students need to be able to both talk *with* others and *to* others in English.

All the activities involve speaking in one way or another. However, they also often incorporate other skills such as reading and writing, both for their own sake and also to provide a basis for oral work.

Using the book

The most important thing to remember in using the materials in this book is that the focus should be on fluency rather than accuracy. It may sometimes be necessary to help the students to understand the vocabulary used in the activities, but the teacher should always avoid putting words into the mouths of the students. They must think of their own ideas and work out how to express them for themselves.

Here is some more specific advice about how to use the book:

1 *Make the students fully aware of the aim of the materials*

2 *Choosing which activities to do*
We suggest you select from the materials those that you think will capture *your* students' interest and present a reasonable linguistic challenge to them. You do not have to do all the units nor do you have to do them in the order that they are presented in the book. It would make sense, however, to do several activities from a single unit in succession as this will enable the students to explore a particular theme in some depth.

3 *Preparing the students to do an activity*
Wherever possible you should avoid extensive preparation of an activity. Do *not* try to teach the students the English you think they will need to talk about a topic. However, sometimes it may be necessary to check that the students understand key vocabulary items in an activity. Vocabulary is a lot more important for talking fluently than grammar! Where you think it is necessary to deal with vocabulary, you can either teach it yourself or ask the students to prepare for an activity themselves by using a dictionary.

The most important part of the preparatory work for an activity is to make sure that students understand what they have to do. You may have to explain instructions to them. If possible do this in English, even if it takes longer. Sometimes, however, it may be necessary to use the students' mother tongue.

4 *Organizing the students for an activity*
Nearly all the activities involve the students talking with each other — in pairs, small groups or larger groups. You need to know what kind of classroom organization is required for each activity and to have thought how best you can organize the students for it. If you are not used to pair and group work do not be put off if at first you experience problems. It takes practice and experience to organize these. One important tip — always make sure that the students are positioned in such a way that they can talk to each other *easily*. Three students sitting in a straight line does not make for easy communication!

5 *During the activities*
An activity is working if the students are talking in English on the topic and are enjoying themselves. If you see that this is taking place, there is no need for the teacher to do anything. In fact, there is a good case for the teacher keeping clear of pair and group work unless something goes wrong. The students may feel freer and so be more prepared to take the risks necessary for speaking in English. If the teacher does sit with a group, he or she should try to participate as a member of the group rather than as teacher. He or she should avoid correcting the students' English as this will make them conscious of *how* they are speaking rather than *what* they are saying.

Things can go wrong during pair and group work. The students may have misunderstood the instructions. They may not know a key vocabulary item needed for the activity. They may find the effort of talking in English too much and switch into their mother tongue. The teacher's role is to facilitate the activities by clarifying instructions where necessary, telling the students any word they ask for and encouraging them to try to use English, no matter how difficult or frustrating they find it at first. One way of getting the students to use English when the teacher finds that they are resisting it, is to let them first explain their idea in their mother tongue and then ask them to collaborate in finding a way to say it in English.

Obviously not all activities will go on for the same length of time. If an activity goes well, it should be allowed to continue and expand. Conversely, if the students' response is limited, for whatever reason, the activity should not be prolonged unnecessarily.

6 *After the activities*
Sometimes the teacher might like to ask the students to reflect on how well they have done an activity. They can mention any particular problems they experienced and these can be discussed in class. This reflection is made easier if the teacher has recorded some of the group work. The recordings can be played back and serve as a basis for discussion. Sometimes there are reflection activities in the units themselves, but the teacher should feel free to introduce reflection whenever he or she feels it is beneficial. Reflection provides the opportunity for some formal correction, although it should also consider other issues — how well the students in a group worked together and whether any interesting ideas emerged, for instance.

The Teacher's guide

At the back of the book there is a Teacher's guide. This provides some answers to the more closed of the activities and also some advice about how to approach specific activities.

Nationalities

1 People of the world

Task 1

In groups write down all the countries that you have visited or would like to visit.

Talk about the differences between the countries.

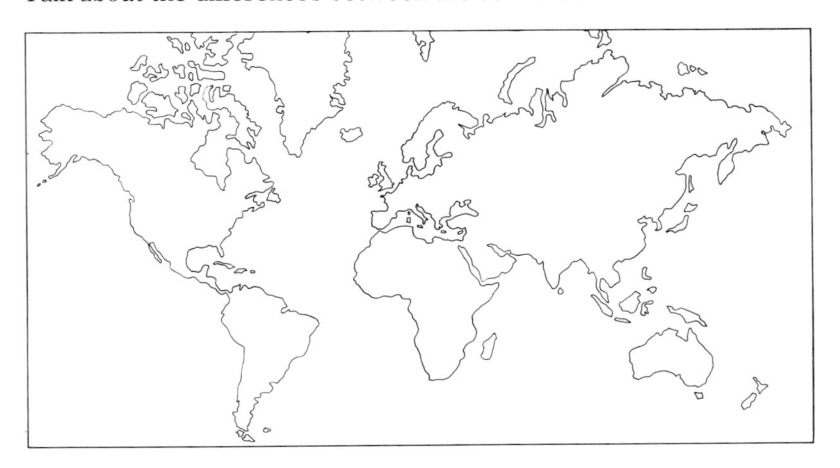

Task 2

In groups write down the English names of as many nationalities as you can think of.

Group the nationalities under the following headings:

European	South American
African	Central American
Asian	West Indian
North American	South Seas.

Task 3

What do you think are the main differences between any of the following?

the English and the French
the Nigerians and the Indians
the Australians and the Germans
the Americans and the Russians
the Chinese and the Italians.

Task 4

Look at the following pictures and for each one say:

- Where the people come from.
- What the picture tells you about the country.

1 2 3 4 5 6

Find other pictures of people from different countries.
Ask other groups to tell you where the people come from and what the pictures tell you about the countries.

2 Countries

Task 1

Form pairs and sit back to back.
In each pair decide who is Student 1 and who is Student 2.

Student 1 should think of a picture of one of the following countries:

England
Italy
USA
France
Australia

Student 1 should give instructions to Student 2 to draw the picture he/she is thinking of. Student 2 can ask questions but Student 1 cannot look at the picture until it is finished.

When the picture is finished Student 2 should find a different Student 1 and sit back to back with him/her.

Student 2 should look at the picture in front of him/her and then give instructions to the new Student 1 to draw an exact copy of the picture. Student 1 can ask questions but cannot look at Student 2's picture. When the picture is finished the pair should look at both pictures and talk about the differences between them.

Put all the pictures on the wall. In groups decide which country each picture is about.

Tell the class why you made your decision about each picture.

In groups write two sentences to describe each of the countries above.

3 Your country

Task 1

How true a picture of the English does the cartoon opposite give?

Think about your country, the people from your country and the ideas that other people have about them.

Tell the other members of your group or class what ideas you think other people have about people from your country. Do you agree with them?

Task 2

In groups discuss the following statement:

'People from different countries are not really very different from each other.'

Discuss your conclusions with another group or with the whole class.

4 A world government

Imagine that it is now the year 2100 and that there are no longer lots of different governments in the world. Instead there is a world government consisting of two people elected from each country.

Task 1

In groups discuss the policies that you would like the world government to follow. Use the following headings to help you:

Taxes
Development
Unemployment
Health
Equal rights
Pensions
Education

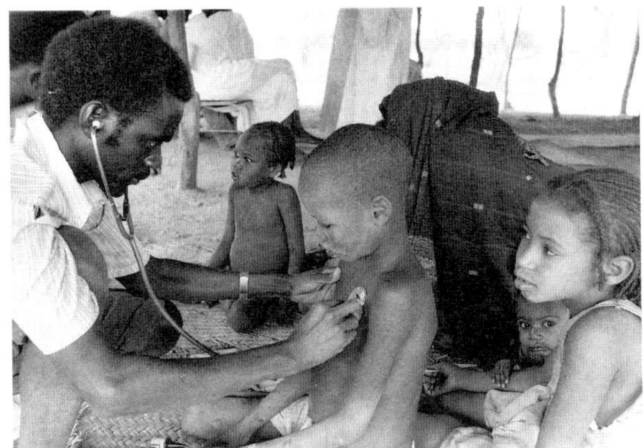

Task 2

With the help of your teacher write on the board ten principles for the world government to adopt, e.g. *The government should create jobs.* Which do you think are the most important?

2 Travel

1 Advertisements

Task 1

Look at the advertisement below and then answer the questions in groups.

- What is the advertisement trying to get people to do?
- Why is there a watch joining England and France?
- What do the following sentences mean?
  'It's quicker by miles.'
  'Calais brings the continent closer.'
- What are the main advantages of travelling from England to France by sailing from Dover to Calais?
- What are the disadvantages?

Task 2

Imagine you are going to travel from London to Paris for a holiday. Think about the different ways you could use to get to Paris and decide which one to take.

Tell another group about your decision and explain why you made it.

Task 3

It is planned to build a tunnel under the English Channel to join England and France by railway.

Imagine that the tunnel is now built and design an advertisement to persuade people to use it.

Task 4

The pictures below are taken from an advertisement.

In groups decide what is being advertised.

Why do you think the advertisers use the word 'unforgettable' under both pictures? Why do they mention the $3\frac{1}{2}$ hours for Concorde and the 5 days for the QE2?

Write the text for the advertisement.

Keep your description short and simple. It must persuade people to make the journey that you are advertising.

Task 5

Find some travel advertisements and think about how they try to persuade you to do something.

Form groups.

Show your advertisements to the others in your group and discuss how they try to interest and persuade people.

Decide on an interesting journey you would all like to make.

Design an advertisement to persuade people to make the journey using a particular form of transport.

Show your advertisement to another group and ask them to help you to improve it.

Produce a final copy of your advertisement and then pin it on the wall.

Discuss the other advertisements on the wall and decide which you think is the best one.

Tell the class which one you have chosen as the best and explain why you have chosen it.

2 Steam trains

Task 1

Look at the photograph below of Mallard, a steam locomotive.

Answer the following questions in groups.

- Mallard was a Pacific class locomotive. All Pacific class steam locomotives were 4-6-2s. Look carefully at the photograph and try to work out what 4-6-2 means.
- Mallard broke the record in 1938. Why do you think no steam locomotive has ever broken this record since?

Task 2

In most countries of the world, trains are now pulled by diesel or electric locomotives. In groups decide which of the following reasons persuaded people to stop making steam locomotives.

- Steam locomotives get very dirty.
- An electric or diesel locomotive only needs a driver but a steam locomotive needs one man to drive it and another man to put the coal or wood on to the fire.
- Steam locomotives are not as fast as diesel or electric locomotives.
- Steam locomotives are very ugly.
- Diesel and electric locomotives can be used all day long.
- Steam locomotives have to stop to be cleaned out and to take on more coal and more water.
- It is cheaper to use diesel oil or electricity than it is to use coal or wood.

Mention any other reasons you can think of why many countries decided not to use steam locomotives anymore.

Task 3

In 1968 British Railways stopped using steam locomotives. Many people were very sad.

Was it because:

- It cost more to travel by train.
- They enjoyed watching steam locomotives and found diesel and electric locomotives very boring.
- Many railwaymen lost their jobs.
- They thought diesel and electric locomotives were more dangerous than steam locomotives.

3 Stories

Task 1

In groups make up a story about an exciting journey by train.

When you have made up your story tell it to the teacher and ask him/her for suggestions to improve it.

Practise telling your story again and then tell it to the class with each person in the group telling a part of the story.

Task 2

Look at the following beginnings of short stories:

'Last year I drove across the Sahara Desert.'

'I'll never forget that long, lonely journey across the Atlantic.'

'At last the preparations were over and we were flying to the moon.'

'I usually caught the six o'clock train home but that night I missed it and had to wait for the seven o'clock train.'

Decide which of the short stories you want to write and then form a group with three or four people who want to write the same story, and sit in a circle.

Copy down the first sentence of the story on a piece of paper.

Write a second sentence for the story.

Pass your piece of paper to the person on your right and take the piece of paper from the person on your left.

Read the two sentences on your new piece of paper and then write a third sentence.

Pass the piece of paper to the person on your right, take the piece of paper from the person on your left, read the three sentences and then write a fourth sentence.

Carry on writing sentences and passing the stories on until you receive a piece of paper which has twelve sentences on it.

Write an ending for the story in front of you.

As a group look at the stories you have written and decide which is the best one.

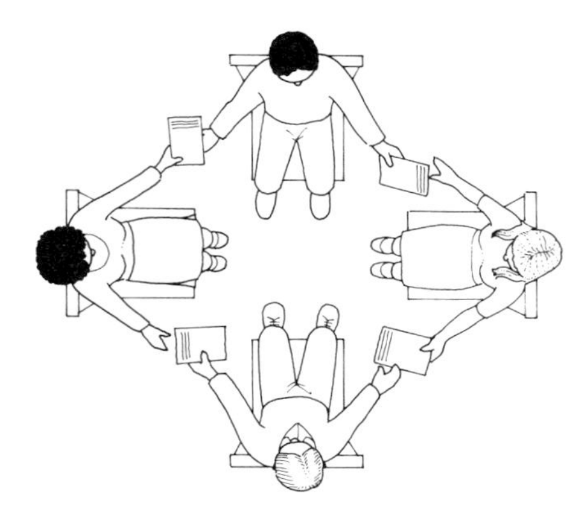

Re-write your best story to make it as accurate and interesting as possible.

Practise telling the story by taking it in turns to tell parts of it.

As a group tell your story to another group and answer any questions they ask you about it.

4 Vehicles

Task 1

Look at the advertisement for the Sinclair C5, a new battery-driven vehicle.

This is the remarkable Sinclair C5. Practical personal transport—powered by electricity.

It's a world first.

It needs no petrol, just an overnight charge from a mains socket.

Anyone fit to be on the roads can drive it, from the age of 14 upwards.

You need no licence, no helmet. You pay no road tax.

The power for 20 miles costs you less than 5p.

Most remarkable of all is its price, just £399.

Above all, it's available now—in production already at the rate of thousands a month. The revolution in the way you travel has begun.

In pairs complete the following table about the Sinclair C5.

THE SINCLAIR C5

Good points	*Bad points*
1	1
2	2
3	3
4	4
5	5
6	6

Task 2

You need transport to get to work in a busy city. You have £500 to spend on a vehicle. Decide whether to buy a C5, a second-hand car, a motorbike or a bicycle.

Give reasons for your decisions.

Find a pair which has made a different decision from you and try to get them to change their minds.

Task 3

In groups design the C6, an improved version of the C5 which costs £499.

Show and describe your design to the class.

Task 4

You live in Saba and you work for companies which make vehicles.

The government of Saba has decided to give a lot of money to the company which designs the best vehicle.

Form groups and give your group a company name. Then work together to design a revolutionary new vehicle for Saba which will help solve many of the transport problems in the country.

When designing the vehicle think about the following:

- Saba is very hot.
- It is also very crowded.
- Most people do not have enough money to buy a vehicle.
- The roads are very bad.
- There are many rivers and lakes.
- There is no oil or coal.
- There are lots of forests.
- Saba has very heavy rains for most of the year.
- It is a small country and most people do not have to travel far.

When you have made decisions draw a detailed plan of the vehicle.

Practise explaining how your vehicle works and giving reasons why your company should get the money from the government.

Task 5

Show your drawing to the class and explain the advantages of your vehicle. Answer any questions from the class about how your vehicle works, what it is made from, how much it will cost, how it is powered (by petrol/electricity/diesel), why it is a good vehicle for Saba.

Which group's vehicle is the best for Saba? Explain why the government should give the money to the company which has designed it.

Task 6

The Flyda is a new transport system which is going to be built in Cardiff, the capital city of Wales.

In groups look at the diagram below and decide how the new system works and why it is a good system for a big city.

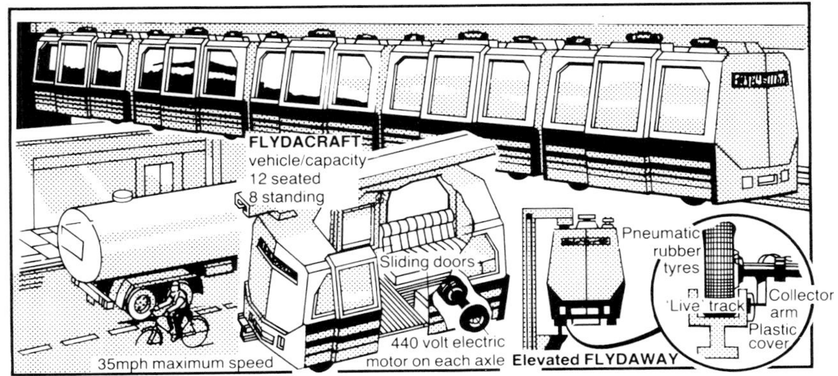

All change: Inside the Flydacraft, and how the new sytem will work

Imagine that you are the inventors of the Flyda system. Choose a big city that you know and write a letter to the city council to try to persuade them to build a Flyda system in their city.

Task 7

In pairs invent a new transport system for a city that you know. Draw diagrams of your system and then explain how it works to other pairs or to the class. Answer any questions about how your system works, what it is made from, what its advantages and disadvantages are.

3 Sport

1 Rules

Task 1

Choose one of the following sports. Think about how you would explain it to someone else.

handball
volleyball
water polo
badminton
rugby
hockey

Form a group with other students that have chosen your sport. Practise telling the class how to play it.

Think about how you will answer questions which people might ask.

As a group tell the class how to play your sport. Tell them about the rules and what you need to do to win. Answer any questions.

Afterwards think about your instructions to the class and decide how you could have made them clearer.

Task 2

As a group choose one of the following 'new' sports (they do not really exist). Invent the rules and the method of scoring.

highball
head tennis
keep ball
football golf
touch ball

Form a pair with somebody from another group which has chosen a different sport. Teach your sport and learn to play your partner's sport.

Now discuss with your partner how you could improve the teaching of your sport. Choose one of your sports and teach it to another pair.

Task 3

In groups of four choose one of the sports above and practise miming it (playing it without speaking and without using any equipment).

As a group mime your sport to the class. The other groups decide which sport they think it is and write it down and give reasons for their decision.

When all the groups have mimed their sport, each group tells the class which sport they mimed and what they were doing in their mime. Each group then adds up all its right answers and the group with the most right answers is the winner.

2 Rise to fame

Task 1

In groups make up a story which connects the three photographs below.

Tell your story to the class.

Task 2

Find sports photographs in magazines or newspapers and bring them to class.

As a group choose any four photographs and ask another group to make up a story connecting them.

Tell your story to the class.

3 Crossword

In groups try to do the sports crossword below.

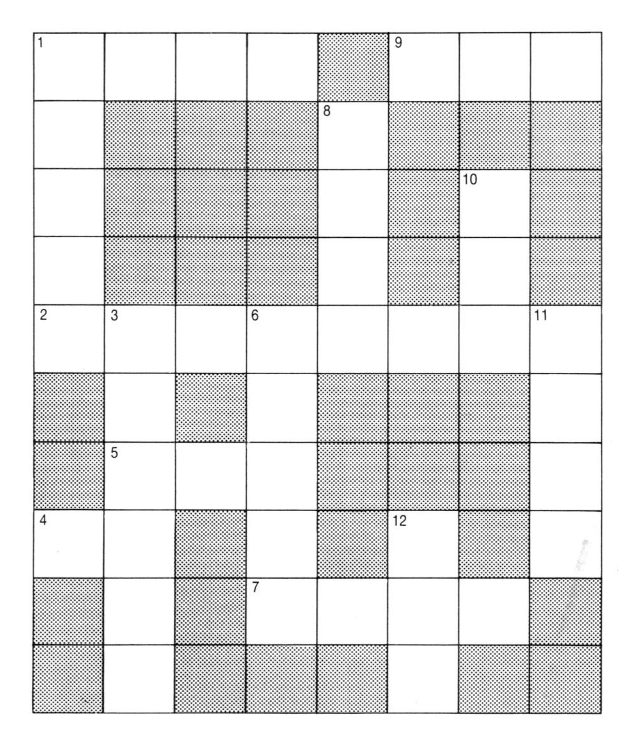

CLUES

DOWN

1 He won four gold medals in the Los Angeles Olympics (1984).
3 The player who scores the most points.
6 You can get one if you win.
8 They play together against another one.
10 You do it at the beginning of the long jump, the high jump and the javelin events.
11 You try to get at least one of these in hockey, water polo and soccer.
12 You use one to hit the ball in baseball and cricket.

ACROSS

1 Brazil did this in the World Cup in Spain in 1982.
2 A sport which gets you wet.
4 You need to get . . . . . . to do 2 across.
5 You can do this to say 'yes' or you can do it with your head to a football.
7 You do this to the other team if you are winning and you are 'in it' if you are winning a race.
9 You try to put the ball in this to get an 11 down.

4 Sporting definitions

Task 1

In groups look at the pictures and definitions below and then try to match them in the table. Some pictures have no definitions which are connected to them.

Give reasons for your answers.

Write definitions for the pictures which have no paragraphs connected to them. Use your dictionary.

picture	a	b	c	d	e	f	g	h
definition								

c

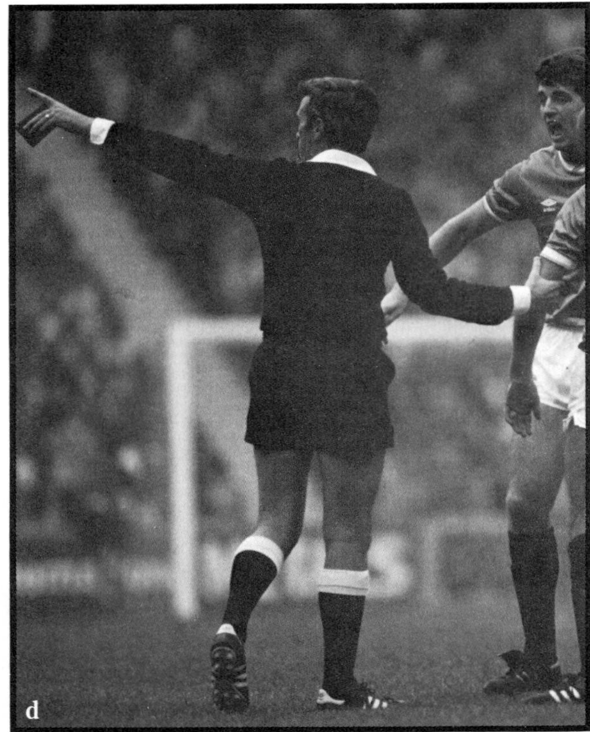
d

e

f

g

h

1 Curling. 1. Scottish game played on ice or other smooth frozen surface with large stones which are hurled along a rink towards a tee; stone used in this, of polished granite, cheese-shaped, and not more than 36in. in circumference or 50 lb. in weight, with an iron or wooden handle on the upper surface. 2. —, iron, — tongs, tongs for curling the hair.
2 Starting-block. Shaped block for bracing the feet of runners at start of race. The invention and use of starting-block has given runners, and especially those in short-distance sprints, the benefit of additional traction when the gun is fired.
3 Javelin. Light spear thrown with the hand. Javelin throwing was a field event in the ancient Olympics as well as in the modern Games.
4 Baseball. National field-game of U.S., played between two teams of nine players on a diamond-shaped field with four bases round which the batter runs in order to score; ball used in this game. To score runs in baseball, the batsmen must hit the ball pitched to them and complete the circuit of bases as many times as possible.
5 Hockey. Field-game played with a small hard ball and with sticks hooked or curved at one end between two teams of eleven players on each side having the same positions as in association football, the object being to drive the ball through the opponents' goal; ice-form of hockey played on ice with each side having six players on skates and with puck instead of ball.
6 Referee. Arbitrator, person to whom dispute is to be or is referred for decision; umpire, esp. in football. v. act as referee (for), esp. in football.

Task 2

Choose pictures of two sports you do not know much about and try to find out more about how they are played. Ask friends or try to find the sports in books.

Be prepared to explain to the class how these sports are played.

Task 3

Select three of the pictures and then challenge another group to describe them and to answer your questions on them. Give marks out of ten for each picture based on how clearly you think the group explained the picture. Tell the group why you have awarded each mark.

1 What makes you laugh?

In this unit we will be looking at ways of making people laugh and at what different people find funny.

Task 1

Look at the list below and tick those things which make you laugh.

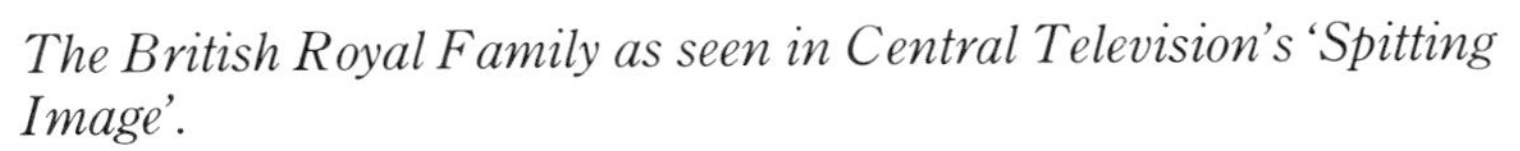

The British Royal Family as seen in Central Television's 'Spitting Image'.

- Comedy programmes on television which make fun of famous people
- Very clever jokes
- People with funny faces
- Jokes about sex
- Cartoons on television
- Puppet shows
- Films in which everything goes wrong
- Comedians imitating famous singers
- Plays in which the characters do ridiculous things
- Ridiculous things happening in real life

Compare your list in groups. Tell each other why some of the things on the list make you laugh and why some of them do not.

Tell each other about other things that make you laugh.

Task 2

In groups tell each other about films, books, plays, people, television programmes and real-life events which have made you laugh.

Now tell each other jokes and stories which have made you laugh.

After each joke or story talk about why the group laughed or did not laugh.

Task 3

In your group think of different ways to make the other groups laugh (for example, funny faces, funny walks, jokes, funny drawings, mimes, short scenes from plays).

Practise two ways which you are going to use to try to make another group laugh. When you are ready join another group and try to make them laugh. Afterwards talk to the other group about why they did or did not laugh at you.

Try to make your two activities funnier and then try to make another group laugh.

Choose one of your activities. Talk about ways of making it funnier, practise it and then use it to try to make the whole class laugh.

2 Nationality jokes

In many countries jokes are told about a particular nationality. In Britain a lot of jokes are told about Irishmen.

Task 1

Form pairs and decide who is Student 1 and who is Student 2 in the group.

Student 1 should read only Irish joke A.

Student 2 should read only Irish joke B.

Students 1 and 2 should tell each other their jokes and try to make each other laugh.

A **Englishman** Have you heard the story about the Irishman who went to the moon?
Another Be careful. That big guy standing next to you at the bar is Irish.
Englishman It's all right. I'll tell the story slowly.

B **Irishman** Now Mick, just dig a deep hole in the road here.
Another And what will I do with the earth that I dig out of the hole?
Irishman Just dig another hole and bury it.

Look at the jokes together and discuss what you like and what you do not like about them.

Do you have similar jokes in your country? Tell each other any jokes you know about other nationalities.

Task 2

In groups discuss the following statements:

'It is wrong to tell jokes about people from other countries.'
'It is natural and harmless to make jokes about people from other countries.'

Make up a group statement saying what you think about jokes which laugh at people from particular countries. Show your statement to another group and ask them to give their opinion about it.

Task 3

Cartoonists often draw characters in their cartoons so that everyone will know what country they come from.

In groups draw a funny character from each of the following countries:

Australia	France
Germany	England
China	Scotland
Russia	USA
Italy	Spain

When you have finished show your drawings to another group. Ask them to decide which country each of your characters is from and give reasons for their decisions.

3 Riddles

Task 1

In pairs look up the meaning of 'riddles' in a dictionary.

Think of examples of riddles in your own language and explain them to your partner.

Try to find or make up riddles in English.

Get another pair to try to answer them.

Do the following crossword in pairs. The clues are nearly all riddles.

DOWN
1 What grows bigger when you take more from it?
4 What do apes have which no other animals have? (two words)
6 What will a white stone become if you throw it into the Red Sea?

ACROSS
2 What has teeth but does not eat?
3 You sometimes do this if you find a joke just a little bit funny.
5 What kind of ears does an engine have?

4 Cartoons

Task 1

Look at the cartoons. In each one a word has been missed out.

a

"Can I borrow the tonight, Dad?"

"What's your name? I need it for the .."

"Know what I miss, Lennie? I miss the

"Waiter, there's a eating my soup!"

In groups decide what the missing word is.

When you have finished compare your cartoons with those of another group and decide which are the funniest.

Task 2

In groups draw cartoons using the following captions:

'These flowers taste delicious.'
'I've put the door out and locked the cat.'
'I told you it only needed a little push.'

Show your cartoons to another group and explain anything they do not understand.

5 Fiction

1 Animal fables

Task 1

In groups discuss stories that children in your country read about animals. Do these stories teach the children lessons or are they just for pleasure?

Look at the picture below. It is from a book which tells a well-known animal story. What are the animals in the story?

What do you think the story is about?

Look at the pictures below and on the next page. They tell the story of *The Rabbit and the Tortoise*. Talk about the pictures and then tell the story by taking it in turns to make up sentences.

Write the story of *The Rabbit and the Tortoise* for young children. Make sure that your story is easy enough for them to understand.

Now make up a story about *The Rabbit and the Tortoise* for adults. Try to make your story funny and critical of modern life.

Choose one of the following ways in which to present your story to the class.

- Present your story as a series of drawings and captions (sentences written under the drawings). You can use some of the drawings above if you want.
- Present your story to the rest of the class with one of you telling the story while the other members of the group mime the action (act the story without speaking).
- Write your story as a short play. Practise reading it aloud and then perform it for the class.

Task 2

As a group make up a new fable about modern life in your country and then present it to the class in any way you want to.

Help the other groups to correct and improve their stories and listen to their suggestions for your story. Check the past tenses of verbs in your course or grammar book, check spellings in your dictionary and make sure your sentences end with a full stop and begin with capital letters.

Write out the final copy of your story, draw pictures to go with it and then pin the story and the pictures to the wall for the other groups to read.

2 Old age

Task 1

Look at the following photographs of old people.

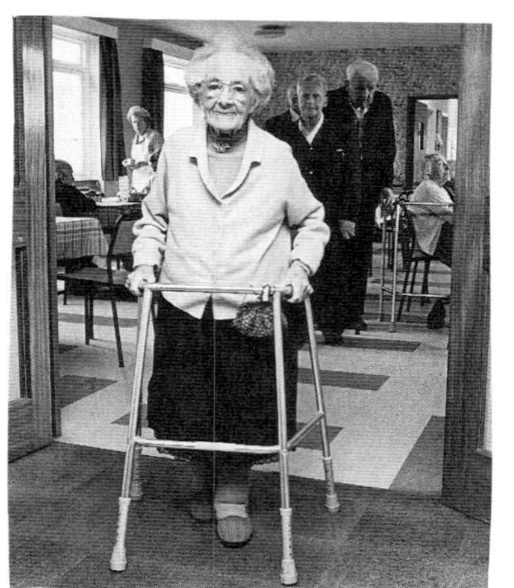

In groups talk about the people in the photographs and decide how they are similar and how they are different.

Now describe and talk about old people that you know. Use some of these phrases to help you:

Most old people . . .
Some old people . . .
Old women like . . .
Old men do not . . .
I like old women who . . .
I do not like old men who . . .

Try to make the sentences connect with each other, for example:

Many old people are lonely. But some like to be alone. rather than
I like old men who tell stories. Old men like to shout at children.

Task 2

Your teacher is going to read a poem about an old lady. Write down five words you think might be in the poem. Show your words to a partner and say why you expect to find them in the poem.

Think of an old lady. What does her face look like? Does she look happy? What colour is her hair? What is she wearing? What is she doing?

Close your eyes and picture the old lady. Watch her carefully while your teacher reads the poem to you.

Discuss the following questions with your group:

- Is the old lady happy? Why?
- Do you like her?
- Do you know anybody similar to her?
- What does she want most?

Phineus:
I'm an old old lady
And I don't have long to live.
I am only strong enough to take
Not to give. No time left to give.
I want to drink, I want to eat,
I want my shoes taken off my feet.
I want to talk but not to walk
Because if I walk, I have to know
Where it is I want to go.
I want to sleep but not to dream
I want to play and win every game
To live with love but not to love
The world to move but me not move
I want I want for ever and ever.
The world to work, the world to be clever.
Leave me be, but don't leave me alone.
That's what I want. I'm a big round stone
Sitting in the middle of a thunderstorm.
There you are: that's true.
That's me. Now: you.

Task 3

Do one of the following with other people from the class:
- Practise reading the poem aloud by two different women.
- Paint pictures of the 'old lady'.
- Write the old lady's diary for this week.
- Pretend you are members of the old lady's family and decide what you think should happen to her. Should she come to live with you/ go into a home for old people/get an old person's flat/live by herself?

- At the end of the poem the old lady says:
  'That's me. Now: you.'

  Write a poem about yourself and then ask other people who have written poems to help you to improve it.

Present your work to the class, for example show your pictures and answer questions about them; read the poem in different ways and ask the class to talk about the differences; tell the class what you have decided about where the old lady should live.

3 Book covers

Task 1

In groups talk about what makes a good cover for a paperback book.

Look at the three book covers below and decide which you think is the best. Make sure you can give reasons for your decision.

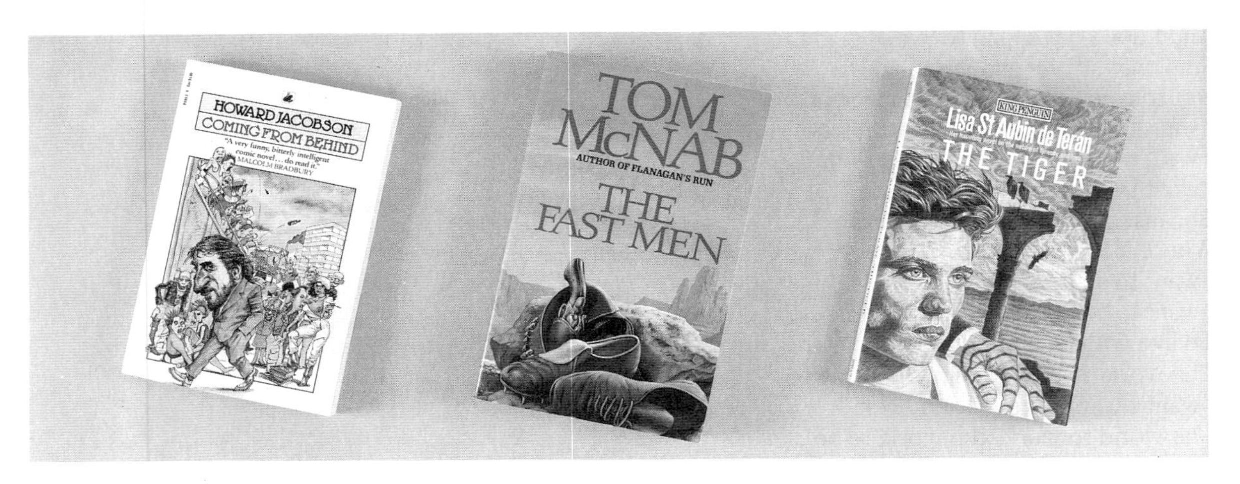

Choose one of the book covers and try to work out what happens in the book.

Tell the class about the book you have chosen. Tell them who you think the people in the book are and what they do. Try to make people want to read the book.

Task 2

Design a book cover for one of the following titles:

An Ice-Cream War
Joshua Then and Now
Weep in the Sun
Midnight's Children
The Restaurant at the End of the Universe

Help the teacher to judge which group has designed the best book cover.

4 Science fiction

Task 1

Read the passage and as you read try to answer the following questions:

1. Where does the story take place?
2. When does the story take place?
3. Who is Miranda?
4. Who is Varon?
5. Who is Garth?

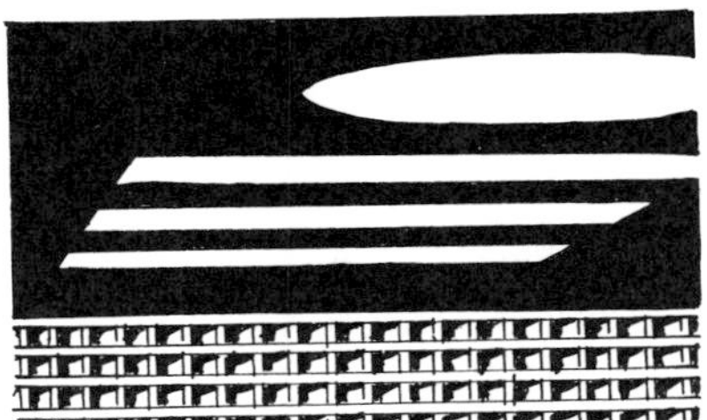

Miranda went to one side of the control room and touched a button. The door of the safety room slid open. Miranda went inside and closed the door. She had a plan of her own.

The large blue capsules were on the tray which had come out of the wall. Miranda picked up a capsule and opened it carefully. It was full of white powder. She emptied the white powder into some water. Then she poured the liquid into an injection gun.

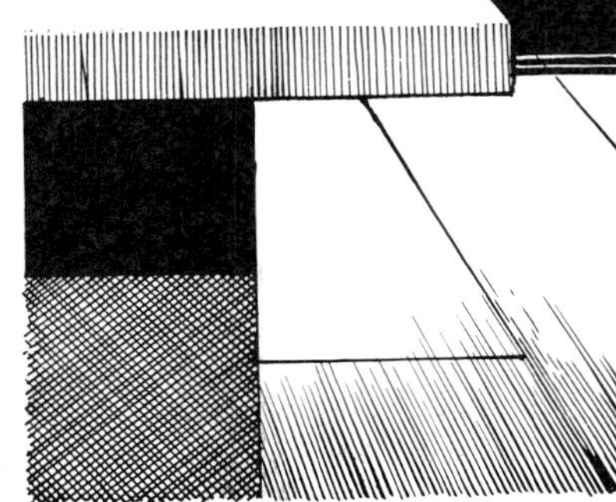

Miranda put the gun carefully into a pocket in her overalls. She now had a weapon of her own.

'Garth will not think of searching me,' Miranda said to herself. 'He doesn't know I have a different plan for the crystals.'

Miranda went back to the control room. Omega was silently charging the power banks. The visual display showed the sleeping bodies of Garth and Varon.

'When will the ship be ready to leave for Zeron?' she asked Omega eagerly.

'In three and a half hour's time,' was Omega's reply.

'Keep watching Garth,' Miranda ordered. 'But you can stop watching Varon. He is locked in his cabin. He cannot get out until I open the door.'
'It will be done,' Omega answered.
He pressed the button on the control panel. The picture of Varon disappeared and the picture of the sleeping body of Garth filled the screen.

MORE PLANS

Miranda went out into the corridor and walked the short distance to Varon's cabin. She touched a button in the wall and the door opened immediately. Varon was lying asleep on the bunk.
Miranda looked down at him.
'You're a fool,' she thought. 'How can you lie there sleeping? Anyone who trusts Garth is a fool.'
She shook Varon by the shoulder until he woke up.
'What's wrong?' he asked sleepily. 'Are we ready to leave?'
'Not yet,' replied Miranda. 'I have come to talk to you. I want you to help me.'
'I am going to help you to get the Zeron crystals. What more help do you want?' asked Varon.
'You know very little about me and Garth,' began Miranda.
'I know enough,' interrupted Varon. 'You are thieves. And you are murderers!'
'I am not a murderer,' said Miranda. 'I helped Garth on Earth. But I did not kill the owner of this spaceship.'

The Space Invaders Geoffrey Matthews

Task 2

In groups discuss the following statements about the passage and say whether you agree with them or not. Give reasons.

1 The story is a true story.
2 Miranda owns the ship that they are travelling on.
3 Miranda is planning to deceive Garth.
4 Miranda told Omega to stop watching Varon because she did not want to be seen talking to him.
5 Miranda is a thief.
6 Miranda and Garth have worked together.
7 Garth is a murderer.

Task 3

In groups work out what you think has happened in the story before this scene and what you think will happen after it. Tell your ideas to another group.

Task 4

In groups write the next page of the story.

6 Jobs

1 Talking about jobs

Task 1

Look at the pictures individually and write down what job each person has.

Take it in turn to say what the people in the pictures *are doing*. Do not say what their jobs are. Let other students guess.

Task 2

Write down the name of each job shown in the pictures. Write down how much each person is paid per year for doing this job in your country. Then write down how much you think each person should be paid.

Job	*Salary paid*	*Salary deserved*
1		
2		
3		
4		
5		
6		
7		
8		

Work with a partner. Tell him or her how much each person is paid. Then say how much you think each person should be paid and say why.

These phrases may help you:

A . . . . . . gets/earns . . . . . . annually/in a year.
I think a . . . . . . should get . . . . . . because . . .
I think . . . . . . in my country are paid too much because . . .
I think . . . . . . in my country are not paid enough because . . .
A . . . . . . is a(n) difficult/easy job because . . .

List the jobs in order of the salary you think they should get. Put the highest-paid job at the top of your list and the lowest-paid at the bottom.

Task 3

One student writes his/her list of jobs on the blackboard and explains the order to the rest of the class. The other students ask questions or make comments.

Task 4

What have you learnt from this task? Make a list of any new words for jobs you have learnt. Was there anything you wanted to say in English but could not? Write down what you wanted to say in your own language. Try and get another student or teacher to help you say it in English.

2 Unusual jobs

Task 1

Look at the picture.

- What is the man doing?
- Do you know what his job is called?
- How much money do you think he earns?
- Do you see people doing this job in your country?

Task 2

The information in the table below is mixed up.

Job	*Description*
undertaker	helps children to cross the road
conductor	improves people's appearances
lollipop lady	performs dangerous acts in films
stunt man	puts people to sleep
plastic surgeon	arranges funerals
anaesthetist	collects bus fares

In pairs match each job to its correct description.

Task 3

What is unusual about the jobs in the table? Do you know any other unusual jobs? Make a list with your partner. If you do not know the name of the job in English, you can write a sentence saying what kind of work the job involves.

When you have finished your list, show it to some other students. Try and find out the names of any of the jobs you did not know.

Task 4

Imagine you are one of the people in the table. You can choose which one. Write out a timetable of a typical day's work. Begin with the time you go to work and end with the time you get back home.

When you have finished, tell your partner about your day's work.

Alternatively, write a story about the person in the picture. When you have finished tell your story to your partner.

Task 5

Choose two jobs from the table — the job you would most like to have and the job you would least like to have. Then fill in a table like the one below, listing the advantages and disadvantages of the two jobs you have chosen.

When you have finished the table, work with a partner and talk about the two jobs you have chosen.

Job	*Advantages*	*Disadvantages*
1		
2		

Task 6

Someone will give a short talk about the job he/she would least like to do and the job he/she would most like to do. Listen to the talk and then complete a table like the one above to summarize what he/she says.

If you do not understand anything that the speaker says, stop him/her and ask questions.

3 Getting a job

Task 1

A big hypermarket is opening up in your town. You are responsible for recruiting staff. In pairs produce an application form which asks for all the information you need, for example, age, qualifications, etc.

Task 2

The following advertisement appeared in a local paper.

Superstore

requires cashiers, store detectives, cleaners, storemen and supervisors for new hypermarket. Ring 567 134 for application form.

Choose one of the jobs mentioned in the advertisement and fill in the application form.

In pairs talk about how you can improve your application.

Task 3

Here are some questions from an interview for the job of store detective in the new hypermarket. Put them in the order you would ask them if you were the interviewer. Then add two questions of your own.

- What do you like doing in your spare time?
- Why have you applied for this job?
- What things about the job do you think you would find difficult?
- Why do you think you are suited to this job?
- Tell me about your family.
- What would you do if you saw someone stealing something in the store?
- What would you like to be doing in five years' time?

In pairs take it in turns to be the interviewer and interviewee for this job.

Task 4

Choose an interview panel of three or four students. Choose three students to be interviewed for the job of store detective. Hold the interviews. When they are over, the panel should discuss the applicants and choose the one they think is best.

Afterwards talk about the interviews. Do you agree with the panel's decision? How could the applicants have done better? Were the interviews fair?

Task 5

Before you read the passage below talk about what a good interviewer should do.

I remember clearly that interview I had with Sir Alexander Walker that day . . .

'Mr Johnson, sit down.' He spoke with a strong Scottish accent.
'Mr Johnson, do ye not find it somewhat impairrtinent to ask for me without an appointment?' Before I could reply, he said: 'I like that in a man. Impairrtinence shows spirit. Now stand up, young man. Walk about. Turrn rround. Look out of the window. How many chairrs are there in the room?'

'Five, sir?'

'How much ash is there on my cigar?'

'About an inch, sir.'

'My tie?'

'Blue, sir.'

'Turrn rround. You are not unobsairrvant. Have you ever been in an adverrtising agency before?'

'No, sir.'

'What made you come heerr?'

'I saw the name, sir.'

'And you recognised it?'

'No, sir.'

'H'mm!!' Then abruptly: 'Would you like me to show ye my agency? Before ye decide to take a job heerr you should see the place.'

'I've already decided, sir.'
'Just the saim I'll show it ye.'
Sir Alexander took me into room after room. He walked with quick steps. He was like a boy showing off his tricks.
At last he took me back to the lift. 'Of course, ye will not be paid a great deal. Ye will receive one pound a week for the fairrst year. After that we shall see.'
I said it was not enough.

One Off T. E. Johnson.

Did you notice anything strange about the spellings in this passage? What are they meant to show?

Answer the following questions in pairs.

1 What job has the man applied for?
2 Where did the interview take place?
3 Who is Sir Alexander Walker?
4 What did Sir Alexander find out about the man?
5 How did he do it?
6 Does this interview seem strange to you? Make a list of all the strange things that happened and explain what makes them strange.

Task 6

Have you ever had an interview? Tell the rest of the class about it. Mention:

- what the interview was for
- where the interview was held
- who interviewed you
- what happened during the interview
- whether the interview was successful
- why you think it was successful/unsuccessful.

Task 7

Fill in the table below with advice on what a good interviewee should and should not do.

Do	*Don't*
be punctual	be late

7 Food

1 Favourite foods

Task 1

Look at the pictures below. They tell part of a story about two animals and their favourite foods. In pairs talk about the pictures and then tell the story.

When you have worked out the story, change partners. Tell your new partner your story and listen to his or hers. Are they the same or different?

Task 2

Here is the story of *Hare and Mosquito*. Read it and then make a list of the differences between it and your own story.

Hare and Mosquito were great friends. One day Hare invited Mosquito to come to his house to eat a meal. When Mosquito came, Hare put a delicious chicken on the table. Mosquito's mouth watered, because it was his favourite food. They washed their hands and then sat down to eat. But Mosquito had a problem. 'My friend, you know I cannot break a piece off the chicken as my hands are not very strong. Can you help me please?'

'How weak you are!' Hare replied. 'The chicken is very well cooked and it is as soft as can be.' Hare ate all the chicken by himself, while Mosquito watched.

When it was time for Mosquito to go home he said to Hare: 'My friend, come and visit me tomorrow. I have collected a lot of honey and I want you to eat it with me.' Hare agreed because honey was his favourite food.

The next day Hare went to Mosquito's house. Mosquito told him to sit down at the table where there was a big jar of honey with a narrow neck. Mosquito dipped his hand into the jar and began to eat. 'Mmm delicious!' he said. But Hare had a problem. 'My friend, you know my hand is too big to go into the jar. Can you help me please?'

'But Hare', said Mosquito, 'it is very easy to dip your hand into the jar — like this.' And Mosquito ate up all the honey while Hare watched.

Task 3

The story of *Hare and Mosquito* has a lesson. In pairs decide what the lesson is. When you have finished, tell the rest of the class.

Task 4

Do you know any stories about people or animals and their favourite foods?

Work in a group and tell each other your stories.

Alternatively, think of a well-known story. Mime the story to the rest of the class, and let them guess what it is about.

Task 5

Make a chart like the one below. Then go around the class asking everyone what their favourite food is. When you have finished make a list of foods in order of their popularity.

Name of favourite food	*Number of people*

Task 6

Give a talk about the results of your survey of favourite foods. You can use this framework to help you:

We did a survey of ______ students. We found that ______ was the most popular food. The next most popular food was ______ .

Now give the talk again using a different framework:

A survey of ______ students was carried out. They survey showed that ______ was the most poular food. The next most popular food was ______ . ______ was third in popularity . . .

Task 7

What names of any foods have you learnt? Make a list. Write down their names in your own language.

2 Dishes and menus

Task 1

Which country is famous for the dishes shown in the pictures below? What are the names of the dishes? Can you describe what they are made of? Complete the table in pairs.

1 2 3 4 5 6

Name of dish	*Country*	*Brief description*
1		
2		
3		
4		
5		
6		

Task 2

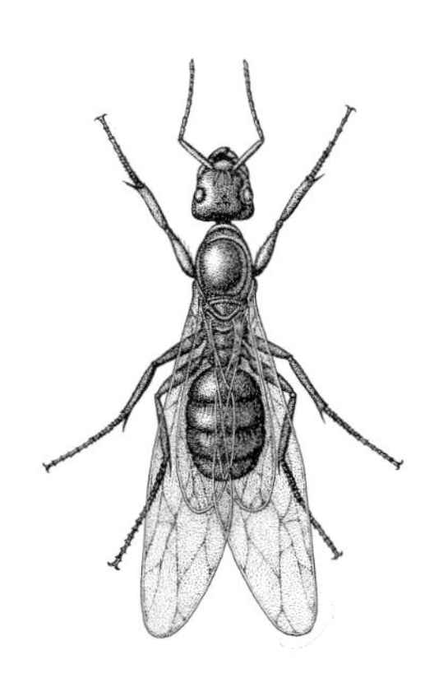

In Central Africa some people are very fond of eating fried flying ants. This is how they are prepared:

Wash the flying ants in water and leave them to dry. Add salt and fry without oil, stirring all the time, until the wings are burnt. Remove them from the heat and fry again in oil.

Would you like to try this dish?

Are there any dishes in your country which foreigners might find unusual? Work with a partner describing how one of these dishes is prepared.

Alternatively, work with a partner to describe how to prepare your favourite dishes.

Task 3

You want to invite some friends for a special meal at your house.

In pairs decide on a menu for the dinner.

Now list all the food and drink you will need to buy and how much they cost.

Menu	*Food*	*Amount*	*Cost*
starter:			
main course:			
dessert:			
drinks:			

Pin up your menus on the wall. Go around and look at the menus prepared by other students. Pick the one you like the most.

Task 4

In pairs find as many different foods as you can. You have three minutes.

P	L	A	I	C	E	B
P	O	R	K	A	H	U
C	H	I	C	K	E	N
M	A	C	E	E	L	U
I	M	E	L	O	N	T

3 Diets

Task 1

Here is a questionnaire about food and diet. Answer the questions to find out how much you know. Compare your answers with your partner's. The correct answers are on page 46.

1 Which foods give us a lot of energy?
  a cereals
  b meat
  c fruit and vegetables

2 Which foods help to build our bodies?
  a cereals
  b meat
  c fruit and vegetables

3 Which food is most fattening?
  a brown bread
  b boiled potatoes
  c salted peanuts

4 Which foods do we get a lot of vitamins from?
  a cereals
  b meat
  c fruit and vegetables

5 People often damage their health by eating too many:
  a breakfast cereals
  b fatty foods
  c frozen vegetables

6 Which of these foods can also be dangerous to our health?
  a salt
  b tea
  c milk

7 Oranges are good to eat because they contain a lot of:
  a vitamin A
  b vitamin B
  c vitamin C

8 Vitamin C is good for you because it:
- **a** makes your hair grow
- **b** helps to fight colds
- **c** helps you to see in the dark

9 Green vegetables like cabbage need to be cooked:
- **a** thoroughly
- **b** with lots of water
- **c** lightly

10 If you live in a cold climate you need a lot of:
- **a** fat
- **b** bread
- **c** coffee

What's your score?

0–3 You have little idea about what to eat to keep healthy. You need to find out quickly!

4–7 You have some idea about what to eat to keep healthy, but need to improve your knowledge.

8–10 You have a good knowledge of what you should eat and should not eat. But what *do* you eat?

To what extent do ideas on healthy eating differ in your country?

Task 2

Look at the diet below. It shows what a 10-year-old British boy eats in a typical day.

Breakfast

Cornflakes (25 g) with sugar (25 g) and milk ($\frac{1}{4}$ litre) 1 boiled egg

2 slices of toast with butter (25 g)

1 cup of tea with 1 teaspoonful of sugar (25 g)

Lunch

1 pork pie

1 portion of chips

1 portion of beans

1 apple

1 chocolate biscuit

1 glass of milk ($\frac{1}{4}$ litre)

Dinner

1 cup of tomato soup

1 piece of chicken (100 g)

1 tomato

lettuce (3 leaves)

2 potatoes

2 slices of bread and butter (25 g)

1 slice of lemon meringue pie

2 cups of tea and 2 teaspoonfuls of sugar (25 g)

1 chocolate biscuit

Supper

1 slice of toast with cheese (25 g)

1 glass of milk ($\frac{1}{4}$ litre)

Snacks during the day
1 can of lemonade
1 packet of salted peanuts (25 g)

In pairs decide whether this is a healthy diet? What do you think a 10-year-old boy in your country would eat in a typical day?

Task 3

Now write down what *you* eat in a typical day and show your partner. Describe your partner's diet to another pair and tell them what you think about it and how you think it could be improved.

Task 4

When we want to talk about food, we often need to use phrases like: *slice of, cup of.*
Go over the diet above and make a list of these phrases. Then work with a partner and think of some more.

Answers to questionnaire

1a 2b 3c 4c 5b 6a 7c 8b 9c 10a
Give yourself one point for each correct answer.

1 What kind of programme?

Task 1

Look at the picture from a television programme.

- What do you think is happening?
- What is this type of programme called?

Work with your teacher to explain each of these types of programmes:

Quiz show
Current affairs
Documentary
Soap opera
Comedy
Chat show
Play
Film
Sport
Educational
Variety show

Task 2

Have you watched television this week? Write down the names of some of the programmes you watched.

Work in a group. Take it in turn to describe one of the programmes you saw. The rest of the group can then decide which type of programme it is.

When you have finished complete a table with an example of each type of programme.

Type of programme	*Example of programme*
Quiz show	
Current affairs	

Now exchange tables with another group. Do you agree with their examples?

Task 3

Here is a list of programmes on British television. In pairs try to guess what each programme is about.

a *What the Papers Say*
b *Gardener's Calendar*
c *On the Ball*
d *Game for a Laugh*
e *Jemima Shore Investigates*
f *Name that Tune*
g *Home Cookery Club*
h *Morning Worship*
i *The Business Programme*
j *A Vous La France*

Read through the paragraphs below. Try to match each paragraph with one of the programme titles.

1 Talking about the Past. A repeat of last Sunday's lesson in the language course for beginners.
2 This special service to mark the Week of Prayer for Christian Unity, comes from the Roman Catholic Church of St Francis and St Anthony.
3 A topical programme that turns the spotlight on business and finance.
4 TV reporter turned private detective investigates another crime, this time involving a group of writers.
5 Ian St John and Jimmy Greaves talk about today's league matches and give their opinions on tomorrow's *Big Match* between Liverpool and Manchester United.
6 The show where the lucky man or woman can win more than £1200, a star prize and the chance to get a fabulous new car — if he or she can identify popular songs quicker than rivals can.

Task 4

Choose two of the programme titles which have no descriptions and try and write paragraphs for them.

Alternatively, choose two programmes you watch on television and write paragraphs like the ones above to describe them.

2 Watching television

Task 1

Look at the chart. It shows what the favourite type of programme of British viewers is.

In pairs talk about what the chart tells you. Try to give reasons to explain the viewers' preferences.

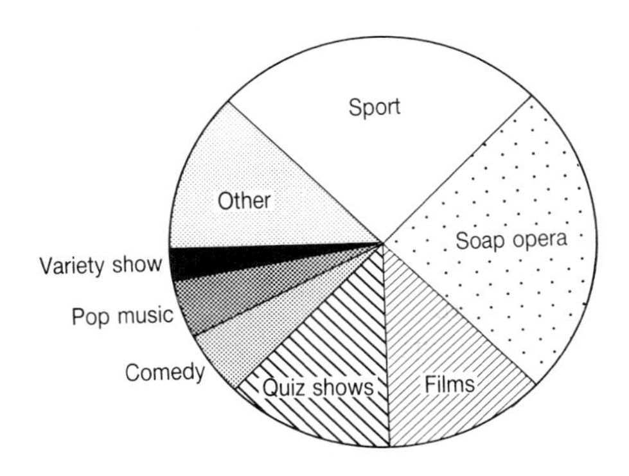

You can use this framework to help you:

The type of programme British viewers like most is . . .
British viewers like . . . . . . more than . . .
British viewers don't like . . . . . . very much.
. . . . . . are most popular because . . .
British viewers prefer . . . . . . because . . .

Task 2

Work in groups of between five to ten students. Take it in turn to say what your favourite type of programme is. As each person answers put a tick in the correct line of the table.

Type of programme	
Quiz show	
Current affairs	
Documentary	
Soap opera	
Comedy	
Chat show	
Play	
Films	
Sport	
Educational	
Variety show	
Cartoons	
Music	
Religious	

When you have finished, add up the scores for each type of programme.

- Which is the most popular type of programme?
- Which is the next most popular?
- How do you compare with British viewers?

Go round each person in your group again. This time each person must say why he/she likes one type of programme more than the others.

In the same groups find out what is the least popular type of programme and why.

Task 3

Here are some statements about children watching television. Which do you agree with? Work in groups of three to four students and try to reach agreement.

YES	NO	
☐	☐	Children watch too much television.
☐	☐	Parents should make sure their children do not watch too much television.
☐	☐	Children like programmes with a lot of violence in them.
☐	☐	Children who like violent programmes are the ones who break the law a lot.
☐	☐	Cartoons are popular because they have a lot of violence in them.
☐	☐	Boys watch television more than girls.
☐	☐	Children watch a lot of television because they are bored.
☐	☐	Children from poor families watch more television than children from rich families.
☐	☐	Children are more likely to watch television by themselves than with their parents.
☐	☐	In general watching television is bad for children.

3 Planning a television schedule

Task 1

British television has four channels:

BBC1	general programmes/sport
BBC2	more educational programmes/documentaries
ITV	general programmes/sport/advertising
Channel 4	general programmes/educational programmes/ programmes for minority groups/advertising.

How many television channels are there in your country?

Are there any differences in the programmes shown on the different channels?

How would you improve the programmes on television in your country?

If you could plan the programmes for a new television channel, what kind of programmes would you like to show?

Task 2

Here is a list of television programmes and the length of each programme.

Programme	*Type*	*Length*
Michael Jackson in Concert	Music	30 mins
African Safari	Documentary about animals	45 mins
Tom and Jerry	Cartoon	15 mins
Dallas	Soap opera	45 mins
This is Your Life	Chat show	30 mins
Panorama	Current affairs	60 mins
News	News	15 mins
Space Travellers	Feature film	120 mins
Double Your Money	Quiz	30 mins
Miss World	Beauty contest	60 mins
Football Special	Sport	45 mins
Athletics	Sport	60 mins
Speak Better English	Educational	30 mins
Story Time	Short story for children	15 mins
Evening Prayers	Religious	10 mins

Imagine that you are in charge of planning an evening's viewing for BBC1. In pairs plan the programmes for Saturday evening from 6.00 p.m. to midnight.

Write out your television schedule like this:

Time	*Name of programme*
6.00 – . . .	. . . .
. . . – . . .	. . . .
. . . – 12.00	. . . .

Task 3

One student gives a talk to the rest of the class about the programme schedule you have prepared.
Give reasons for your choices of programmes and for the times at which you have decided to show them.

Task 4

Work in the same groups and plan another schedule for one of the following:

- Sunday afternoon on a popular channel
- Saturday evening on a popular channel
- an evening schedule for a completely new channel (You will have to decide what kind of channel this will be.).

When you plan your schedule you can use any of the programmes listed above and any other programmes of your own choice.

Task 5

Make a list of the different ways you can use to say what time a programme takes place. For example: *Michael Jackson in Concert starts at 8.00 p.m. and ends at 9.00 p.m.*

Marriage

1 Getting married

Task 1

Here's Simon. He's eighteen. Read what he says.
'I won't get married till I'm thirty or more. When people get married young they usually divorce. They marry for love, but when that dies they find they have nothing in common. They don't have time to find out about themselves or life in general. They have a family before they are ready. Then they feel trapped and blame their partner for all the fun they are missing.'

Simon

David

Here's David. He's eighteen too. But he's got different ideas about marriage.
'I shall get married as soon as I can. When people get married young they . . .'

In groups talk about the reasons David could give for getting married young. Think of at least five and then write them down.

Reasons for getting married young:
1 . . . .
2 . . . .
3 . . . .
4 . . . .
5 . . . .

Hold a class discussion. Work out as many good reasons as you can together for getting married young.

Task 2

Here's Martha. She's eighteen. She's against getting married at all. Read what she says.
'I'll never get married. When a girl gets married she's expected to look after her husband — to cook for him, wash and iron his clothes, keep his house clean. That's not fair. Then when she has children, she has to give up her job and stay at home. Later, when the children are grown up, she can't get a job. A married girl loses all her independence. She stops being a "person" and becomes a "wife".'

Martha

Lizzie

Here's Lizzie. She's eighteen too. But she's got different ideas about marriage. Read what she says.
'I hope I get married. When a girl gets married . . .'

In your groups talk about the reasons Lizzie could give for getting married. Think of at least five and then write them down.

Reasons for getting married:
1 ....
2 ....
3 ....
4 ....
5 ....

Hold a class discussion. Work out as many reasons as possible for getting married.

Task 3

Are you married? If not, do you want to get married sometime?
If so, will it be when you are young or older?

Now think of the reasons for the answers you have given.

In your groups tell each other the answers to the questions and your reasons.

Carry out a class survey on marriage and complete the table below.

No. of students in the class	☐
No. of married students	☐
No. of students who don't want to marry	☐
No. of students who do want to marry:	
before they're 20	☐
between 20–30	☐
over 30	☐

2 Choosing a marriage partner

Task 1

Work with your teacher or with a dictionary. Make sure you understand the words listed below. They all describe personal characteristics.

rich
truthful
independent
considerate
faithful
patient
amusing
intellectual
attractive
sexy
generous
talkative
ambitious
tidy
decisive
broad-minded

Task 2

Choose the six personal characteristics out of those listed which best describe the kind of person you think you are.

1 ....
2 ....
3 ....
4 ....
5 ....
6 ....

Work in your groups or in pairs. Tell each other the six personal characteristics you have chosen to describe yourself. Do you agree with the descriptions of the others in your group? Suggest changes.

When you have finished your discussion make any changes you think are necessary in your self-description.

Task 3

Now work out a description of your ideal marriage partner. Choose the six personal characteristics you would most like to see in your partner.

Write them down.

1 ....
2 ....
3 ....
4 ....
5 ....
6 ....

Compare your lists in pairs and talk about the differences between them.

Task 4

Look back at the list of words in Task 1. Think of an opposite for each word, for example:

rich poor

3 Arranging marriage partners

Task 1

Study these photographs and details about four women and four men.

Check with your teacher that you understand the descriptions.

Decide who you think each woman should marry. Write down the names of their partners.

Sarah should marry ......
Maria should marry ......
Celia should marry ......
Anne should marry ......

Write notes giving the main reasons for your opinions.

Sarah

Maria

Celia

Sarah

Age	21 years
Education	University — BA failed
Interests	Travelling and going to parties
Appearance	Fairly small and very pretty
Personality	Extremely extrovert — loves talking
Job	Unemployed — hopes to work on a fashion magazine

Maria

Age	17 years
Education	Left secondary school at 16
Interests	Reading love stories — going to discos
Appearance	Tall for her age and thin
Personality	Rather introverted — likes to have a laugh
Job	Shop assistant

Celia

Age	29 years
Education	University — BSc honours; also MSc degree
Interests	Going to the theatre and art galleries — holding dinner parties
Appearance	Quite short and on the plain side
Personality	Introvert — but likes to let go sometimes
Job	Studying for PhD

Anne

Brian

Graham

Anne

Age	42 years
Education	Left school at 16 — went to secretarial college
Interests	Visiting friends — walking holidays in countryside
Appearance	Medium build — looks younger than her years
Personality	Extrovert — but can be moody
Job	Personal secretary to company director

Brian

Age	18 years
Education	Has just finished sixth form at school
Interests	Reading and going for country walks
Appearance	Short and stocky
Personality	Introvert — likes being by himself
Job	Student — waiting to go to university

Graham

Age	22 years
Education	University — 1st class honours degree
Interests	Skiing and doing house repairs
Appearance	Tall and good looking
Personality	Generally introvert — but can be lively in male company
Job	Engineer for major construction company

Martin

Philip

Martin	
Age	32 years
Education	Left school at 16
Interests	Playing football and going to the pub with friends
Appearance	Tall and well-built — very fit
Personality	Extrovert — very friendly with everyone
Job	Factory worker

Philip	
Age	45 years
Education	University — BA honours
Interests	Gardening and watching TV
Appearance	Rather short and thin
Personality	Introvert — likes company but not in large groups
Job	Secondary school teacher

Task 2

Work in your group. Tell the others who you think each woman should marry and give your reasons.

Discuss the advantages and disadvantages of the different marriages possible and try to arrive at a group decision on the best arrangement. As you discuss fill in the table.

Woman	*Marriage partner*	*Advantages of marriage*	*Disadvantages of marriage*
Sarah			
Maria			
Celia			
Anne			

One student from each group tells the class what the group has decided, giving the advantages and disadvantages of each arranged marriage.

4 Marriage problems

Task 1

Do magazines and newspapers in your country have Agony Columns?

Discuss the following questions with the whole class.

- What kinds of problems do people write about in an Agony Column?
- What kind of people send in letters to an Agony Column?
- Where can you find an Agony Column?
- Do you think advice from an Agony Column is helpful?
- Why do people like to read Agony Columns?

Task 2

Here is a letter from an Agony Column. Read it carefully and make sure you understand the problem.

> I am a 28-year-old woman with no children. I have been married for 10 years. At first I was very happy with my husband and loved him dearly. But now things have changed. He is very ambitious and spends all his time at work. He also goes abroad a lot. I hardly ever see him.
>
> I am desperate to have a child. But my husband says we should wait longer.
>
> I've become very lonely, so perhaps it's not surprising that when I met another man recently I became interested in him. He is very kind and takes a real interest in me. I think I've fallen in love with him. The trouble is he's a lot older than me — he is 45, in fact. He wants me to go and live with him. But I feel terribly guilty about leaving my husband because I know how upset he will be.
>
> I just don't know what to do, but feel I'm not getting any younger. Can you help?

Work in your group. Talk about the advice you would give to this woman. Together plan and write a response.

When you have finished writing send one member of your group to another group to read them your response. Talk about the response that is read to you. Is the advice the same as you gave or different? Whose advice is better?

Task 3

One student pretends to be the 28-year-old woman in the letter.

The rest of you write down three questions that you would like to ask her to get more information about her and her problem.

The student comes to the front of the class and the rest of you take it in turn to ask her your questions. She must make up answers using her imagination.

Task 4

Work in your group. Talk together and think of a problem you could write about in a letter to an Agony Column. Then plan and write the letter.

Give your letter to another group and read their letter. Talk about the problem in their letter and work out a response.

Task 5

People from different countries deal with marriage problems in different ways. Talk about some of the ways in which marriage problems are dealt with in your country.

Education

1 Changes in education

Task 1

Make a list of the major changes that have taken place in education in your country in the last one hundred years.

Compare your list with that of your partner. Do you think these changes have improved education?

Task 2

Read the description of a school in nineteenth-century England.

Complete this table with a partner. You have to describe what kind of person each one is.

Name	*Kind of person*
Mr Gradgrind	
Cecilia Jupe	
Bitzer	
The government education officer	
Mr M'Choakumchild	

'I want Facts, sir,' said Mr Thomas Gradgrind. 'Teach these children nothing that cannot be proved. Only Facts will ever be any use to them. That is how I bring up my own children, and these children too. Stick to the Facts, sir!'

The scene was a high, plain schoolroom. Mr Gradgrind was a square man with hard dark eyes and a wide, thin mouth. 'In this life,' he said firmly, 'we want nothing but Facts, sir; nothing but Facts.'

The other men listened. In front of them sat forty children, all ready to have Facts poured into them until they were full. Mr Gradgrind pointed to a girl. 'Girl number twenty. Who are you?'

'Sissy Jupe, sir,' said the child, curtseying.

'Sissy is not a name. Say Cecilia.'

'Father calls me Sissy, sir,' replied the girl shyly, curtseying again.

'Then he is wrong. Cecilia Jupe, what does your father do?'

'He works with horses, sir.'

'Very well. What is a horse?'

Cecilia Jupe said nothing. 'There!' said Mr Gradgrind. 'Girl number twenty knows nothing about one of our commonest animals. Bitzer! What is a horse?'

A boy stood up. He looked at Mr Gradgrind with colourless, expressionless eyes. 'Four legs. Eats grass . . . forty teeth . . .' He went on and on.

'Now, girl number twenty,' said Mr Gradgrind. 'You know what a horse is.' She went red, curtseyed, and sat down again.

The third gentleman stepped forward: he was a government education officer. 'Now, children,' he said, 'That is a horse. Would you have wallpaper with horses on it?'

'Yes, sir!' said all the children except one.

'Why wouldn't you do that?' the officer asked this child.

'Please, sir, I wouldn't paper a wall, I would paint it.'

'You must use paper,' said Mr Gradgrind. 'Now children, I will explain why you would not paper a wall with pictures of horses. Do you ever see horses walking up and down your walls?'

'No, sir.' They sounded disappointed.

Of course not,' said the officer. 'You must stick to Facts.'

Thomas Gradgrind looked pleased. 'This is an important thing,' the officer continued. 'I will try again. Would you have a carpet with pictures of flowers on it?' The children knew what he expected now. Most said 'No', and only a few said 'Yes'. Sissy Jupe was one.

'Girl number twenty!' Sissy stood up and curtseyed again. 'So you'd have a carpet with flowers on? Why?'

'Please sir, I like flowers.'

'So you want to put tables and chairs on them, and let people walk on them?'

'Please sir, it wouldn't hurt them. They'd only be pictures; pictures of something very pretty and pleasant. And I'd imagine . . .'

'Imagine!' cried the gentleman. 'You must not do that. You must stick to the Facts, Cecilia Jupe, and forget Imagination. You don't walk on flowers in Fact; so you must not walk on them on carpets. You do not find fruit and birds on your cups and plates in real life; so you must not have pictures of them on your cups and plates. You must have, in simple colours, pictures of mathematical figures which can be proved. That is Fact. This is Taste.'

The girl curtseyed again and sat down. She looked troubled.

'Now,' said the education officer, 'would Mr M'Choakumchild give his first lesson . . .?'

Mr Gradgrind looked pleased. 'We are ready for you, Mr M'Choakumchild.' And the schoolmaster began. He was one of a hundred and forty schoolmasters. They had all been produced at the same educational factory, like a hundred and forty piano legs. They all knew all the Facts about everything. And now Mr M'Choakumchild was ready to deliver all these Facts to the children who sat before him.

Hard Times Charles Dickens (Oxford Alpha Readers)

Task 3

Imagine that you are Mr Gradgrind. Explain why you think the following are wrong:

- papering a wall with pictures of horses
- a carpet with pictures of flowers on it
- cups and plates with pictures of birds on them.

Record your explanations if possible. Then compare them with those in the passage.

Task 4

Either compare your experiences of school with those described in the passage, or describe one of your teachers. Make the description as amusing as possible.

2 Describing your school

Task 1

What is/was your school like? Work with a partner and prepare a description. Talk about some of the following in your description:

- the size of the school
- whether the school is co-educational or single sex
- whether there are separate classes for clever and less able students
- whether there are school fees
- what the minimum school-leaving age is
- whether there is a school uniform
- what happens to less able students
- the school rules.

Task 2

What improvements would you make to your school?

Work in a group and try to agree on the 'ideal school'. Refer back to the list in Task 1.

When you have decided on your 'ideal school' each group presents its description to the whole class.

3 Choosing your own English language programme

Task 1

Imagine that you could choose your own English language programme. What kind of programme would you choose?

Here is a questionnaire to help you describe the programme you would like. Work through the questions by yourself. Then compare your answers with a partner's.

1. How many students would you like in your class?
2. Would you prefer the class to be mixed (i.e. male and female students)?
3. Would you prefer to learn with students of the same age as yourself?
4. How many hours per week would you like to learn English?
5. Do you want to learn all the language skills (speaking, listening, reading and writing)? Are some more important than others?
6. Would you prefer to follow a single textbook or to use several?
7. Would you like the chance to work in a language laboratory?
8. Would you like to do plenty of language drills?
9. Would you like plenty of opportunity to work in groups with other students?
10. Would you like to work with students at the same level of English as yourself or with students of mixed ability?
11. What else would you like in your programme?

Task 2

Prepare a short talk describing the kind of English language programme you would like. You can make use of these expressions:

If I could choose my own language programme, I would . . .
I would prefer . . . . . . to . . .
I would like the opportunity to . . .
My programme would include . . .
It would be better to . . . . . . than to . . .

Give your talk to the rest of the class and be ready to answer questions when you have finished.

4 Comparing language schools

Task 1

Here are descriptions of three language schools in Britain. Read them and complete the table on page 68 in pairs. It will help you to compare what the schools offer.

SCHOOL A

The School was opened in 1955 and is part of a non-profit-making educational foundation. Its 200 students, from 30–40 countries, work in large, attractive buildings set in extensive, beautiful gardens, within easy reach of the centre of Cambridge. The School has dining rooms, a library, video filming studio, language laboratories, listening and self-access study centres, computers, as well as facilities for tennis, table-tennis, volleyball, basketball, badminton and football.

General English classes are for students aged 17 +. Complete beginners are not accepted. Students have classes for 21 hours a week. Other subjects available within the General English timetable include English for Business and English Literature. The cost of tuition, materials and books per term is £1130. Accommodation is with local families. Lunch is provided in the School Monday to Friday. All other meals are taken with the family. There is a full range of social activities including excursions, discos and theatre-visits. The total cost of all non-tuition services is £670 per term. There are 3 terms of 10 weeks and summer courses of 9 weeks and $3\frac{1}{2}$ weeks.

SCHOOL B

This school has a capacity of 220 students. It occupies a 19th century building in a quiet tree-filled square close to Victoria Station in central London.

General courses, either in the mornings or afternoons, comprise fifteen 50-minute periods per week. We cater for a wide range of classes from beginners to advanced, enabling us to place students at the level indicated by the special entry test which all students take. There are usually no more than 14 students in a class. In addition to the fifteen lessons, there are daily individual laboratory sessions and lectures on life in Britain at no extra cost.

There are 8 classrooms, a multi-media learning centre, language laboratory, video, computer, lecture hall, canteen. We are open from January to December for courses of 3 to 14 weeks. There is a special 2-week Easter Course and Refresher Courses for overseas teachers of English in summer. Fees are approximately £46 per week for general courses. Accommodation can be arranged with selected families with half-board. There is a full social programme and regular excursions.

SCHOOL C

This school, founded in 1953, is a non-profit making Charitable Trust. Situated in residential North Oxford, 3 km from the city centre, the College occupies a complex of purpose-built blocks and 14 large victorian houses providing academic and residential accommodation. Facilities include an excellent library, video room, language laboratories, computer room, science laboratories, assembly hall and coffee bar.

A particular benefit for the EFL student is the opportunity to live and study with native English speakers taking the two-year International Baccalaureate course, or courses at university level.

All students are encouraged to participate in social and extra-curricular activities including sports, horse riding, drama, art, crafts, photography, films, concerts and excursions.

Academic Year Courses (21 hours per week) leading to all principal EFL examinations, concentration on language with selected studies in Literature, Politics, History, Art History, Computing. Most students live in college houses each supervised by a resident warden, but some prefer family accommodation.

	School A	*School B*	*School C*
Town			
Kind of buildings			
Number of students			
Facilities for language learning			
Other facilities			
Types of courses			
Length of courses			
Hours per week			
Size of classes			
Type of accommodation			
Social activities			
Cost			

Task 2

Imagine that you are going to Britain to study English. You want to pick a language school. Which language school would you choose?

You can choose one of the three schools described above and give reasons for your choice. Or, if none of the three suits you, you can describe the kind of school you would choose.

When you have made your decision, work with a partner. Tell him/her your decision and ask about his/hers. Make sure you both explain your choices fully.

or
Perhaps you have already studied at a language school in Britain. Describe the school to a partner who has also studied in England.

TEACHER'S GUIDE

UNIT 1

1 People of the world

Task 2
It would be useful to have a good world map in English available to refer to in case of disputes about location, spelling, etc. in Task 2.

It is the discussion that is important in Task 2 not the right answers. However it is important that you adjudicate when necessary and should therefore check up on the spelling and pronunciation of nationalities in English before the lesson.

NB South Seas refers to the islands in the South Pacific, e.g. Tahiti, Fiji, Tonga.

Task 4
The photographs were taken in the following countries:
1 India **2** Kenya **3** England **4** USA
5 Oman **6** France
It is not important that the learners identify the exact country. Any answer is acceptable which is possible from the evidence in the photograph.

2 Countries

Task 1
It is important to check that the learners have understood the instructions by asking the class to watch whilst one pair demonstrates what to do.

4 A world government

Task 1
It is important to check that the learners know the meanings of the headings before and during the group discussion.

UNIT 2

1 Advertisement

Task 2
You could travel from London to Paris by plane (from Heathrow or Gatwick), or by car/coach/train/hitch hiking to a port (Dover, Folkestone or Ramsgate) and then by boat, hovercraft or hydrofoil across the Channel.

2 Steam trains

Task 1
4–6–2 refers to the wheel arrangement (i.e. two small wheels on each side at the front of the locomotive, three large ones in the middle and two small ones at the back).

UNIT 3

1 Rules

Task 1
It would be useful to check up on the rules of the six sports in English so as to be able to help learners if necessary.

Task 2
It is important to stress that these sports are imaginary and that the learners are free to use their imagination in devising rules and methods of scoring.

2 Rise to fame

Task 1
There is no correct answer here but, when the activity is finished, you may like to give students some information on the photographs.

1 The young Bobby Charlton outside his mother's house.
2 Playing for Manchester United in the seventies.
3 Retired soccer star now successful business man.

3 Crossword

Answers:

Down		*Across*	
1	Lewis	1	Lost
3	Winner	2	Swimming
6	Medal	4	In
8	Team	5	Nod
10	Run	7	Lead
11	Goal	9	Net
12	Bat		

4 Sporting definitions

Task 1
a 5 **b** 4 **c** no definition **d** 6 **e** 2 **f** 3
g no definition **h** 1

UNIT 4

3 Riddles

Task 1
Answers

Down		*Across*	
1	Hole	2	Comb
4	Baby apes	3	Smile
6	Wet	5	Engineers

4 Cartoons

Task 1
The actual missing words are:
a car **b** menu
c boos **d** man
However any word which fits is acceptable.

UNIT 6

2 Unusual jobs

Task 1
The man pushing the cart with an assortment of goods on it is *a rag and bone man*. His job consists of calling at people's houses and asking if they have any old clothes or household items that they do not want. A rag and bone man traditionally calls out 'Any old iron' as he moves down a street.

Task 5
Here are some useful phrases for talking about the advantages and disadvantages of the different jobs:
One advantage/disadvantage of being a ______ is that . . .
A ______ earns . . .
The working conditions of a ______ are . . .
A ______ gets a lot of job satisfaction.
A ______ has to . . .

Task 6
You may like to discuss with students how you interrupt somebody who is talking and what you say when you are not clear what somebody is saying. Ask for suggestions from the class and draw up a list on the blackboard.

3 Getting a job

Task 5
The unusual spellings in this passage (e.g. 'impairrtinence') are meant to show that Sir Alexander speaks with a Scottish accent — he rolls his 'r's. You could either ask the students to point out all the unusual spellings or ask them to say the words making them sound Scottish.

UNIT 7

1 Favourite foods

Task 3
Here are some ways of describing the lesson of a story:
From this story we learn that . . .
The moral of the story is . . .
The story tells us that . . .

Task 5
You may want to check that students understand the difference in meaning between 'food' and 'dish'.

Task 6
The two frameworks are noticeably different. The first one is personal (e.g. it uses 'we'). The second one is impersonal and seeks to present an objective report.

You may like to ask students these questions:
What are the differences between the two frameworks?
Which framework is best for giving the results of a survey?

2 Dishes and menus

Task 4
You should be able to find the following names of foods:

PLAICE	PORK
CHICKEN	MACE (a spice)
MELON	HAM
RICE	CAKE
BUN	NUT
ICE	EEL
(= ice cream)	

Students may need to check the meanings of some of these in their dictionaries.

3 Diets

Task 2
You should explain any items in the boy's diet that the students do not know or get them to find out the meanings in their dictionaries.

UNIT 8

1 What kind of programme?

Task 1
Here is a brief description of the different types of TV programmes.

Quiz show This is like a game. There is a questioner and invited people who have to answer the questions. Often a prize is awarded to the winner.

Current affairs These programmes deal with political and social problems, often with interviews. The aim is to give an analysis of the problems and to show different viewpoints.

Documentary This is non-fictional. There is a commentary on the topic, which could be another country, wildlife, a medical issue, etc.

Soap opera Popular soap operas are *Dallas* and *Dynasty*. They are fictional and follow the lives of a group of people. They often try to be sensational.

Comedy This is a fictional programme designed to be amusing. Often it is part of a series about a particular group of people.

Chat show In a chat show there is an interviewer and interviewee, who answers questions about his/her life.

Play This is drama — a special play written for the television.

Film Also drama, but generally made to be shown in the cinema and only afterwards shown on TV.

Sport Programmes that show any sport in action or where people are talking about sport.

Educational Programmes designed to educate people. On British TV there are a lot of schools' programmes on different school subjects.

Variety show This is a programme where different people do acts — singing, telling jokes, dancing, juggling, etc.

Task 3
c 5 e 4 f 6 h 2 i 3 j 1

3 Planning a television schedule

Task 5
Here are some of the ways in which you can say what time a programme takes place:

. . . starts at . . . and ends at . . .
. . . is from . . . to . . .
. . . lasts from . . . to . . .
. . . lasts . . . minutes, starting at . . .
. . . goes on the air at . . . for . . . minutes.
. . . is from . . . to . . .

UNIT 9

2 Choosing a marriage partner

Task 1
Suggested opposites:

rich	poor
truthful	untruthful
independent	dependent
considerate	inconsiderate/selfish
patient	impatient
amusing	boring/dull
intellectual	non-intellectual
attractive	unattractive/plain
sexy	not very sexy (no single word)
generous	mean
talkative	quiet
ambitious	unambitious
tidy	untidy
decisive	indecisive/uncertain
broad-minded	narrow-minded

Task 3
If appropriate to your class, you may like to extend the activity as follows. Ask students to:

Move around the class and try to find your ideal marriage partner from among the other students. You must ask them what their personal characteristics are and tell them what your own are.

You can find more than one partner. Keep a list of all the suitable partners you come across. When you have finished decide on one from your own list. How did you make your final decision?

You may not be able to find a partner with all your ideal characteristics. In this case, find the partner (or partners) who comes closest to your ideal. Write down the name(s).

In turn each student tells the rest of the class who his or her ideal marriage partner is.

4 Marriage problems

Task 1
You will find 'Agony Columns' in many magazines and some newspapers. They consist of letters that readers have sent in with their problems. The writer of the column gives his/her advice. The problems are of a personal nature, often to do with marriage. Sometimes an Agony Column is called a 'Problem Page'.

Task 4
It might be a good idea to elicit from the students a list of typical marriage problems and then write them on the blackboard.

UNIT 10

1 Changes in education

Task 2
The main point to bring out is that Cecilia Jupe is a different kind of person from all the others, because she behaves in a natural, commonsensical sort of way. The others are the 'fact-mongers' — unimaginative, dull, mechanical and lacking in common sense.

Task 3
After the students have completed this task they could be asked to say what they think of Gradgrind's explanations and to try to work out a logical response to them.

2 Describing your school

Task 1
It might help to introduce some vocabulary before the pair work starts:
— co-educational/single-sex
— streamed and mixed-ability classes
— fee-paying (or private) vs free (or state) schools
— minimum/maximum school-leaving age
— high-achieving and low-achieving students
— strict/relaxed discipline

One way to do this is by describing your own school. For example:
'Our school is co-educational. That is there are both male and female students in it. It is not a single-sex school . . .'
Students could be asked to make a note of words with opposite meanings as they listen.

3 Choosing your own English language programme

Task 1
When the students are preparing their answers to the questionnaire individually they should be encouraged to think of reasons. This can be done by asking them to complete a table. For example:

Question	Answer	Reason
1	15 students	More than this would make it difficult for the teacher to give attention to each student.
etc		

4 Comparing language schools

Task 1

Let the students use a dictionary if they want to. Encourage collaboration. Nominate one member of each pair to be 'scribe' and complete the table.

When several pairs have finished, ask them to compare their tables.

The table should look something like this. (Students could compare their tables with this one).

	School A	School B	School C
Town	Cambridge	London	Oxford
Buildings	large and attractive	19th century	purpose-built + victorian houses
No. of students	200	220	—
Facilities for language learning	library, video, lang. labs, self-access study centres	lang. labs, multi-media learning centre, video, computer	library, video, lang. labs., computer
Other facilities	various sports, dining rooms	canteen	science labs., coffee bar, assembly hall
Types of courses	general Eng. (not beginners)	general Eng. (all levels)	general Eng. and specialist courses
Length	one term (10 weeks)	3–14 weeks	1 academic year
Hours per week	21	15 (× 50 mins)	21
Size of classes	—	14	—
Type of accommodation	family	family	College/ family
Social activities	excursions, discos and theatre visits	excursions	film, concerts, excursions (+ other leisure activities)
Cost	£1130 per term	£46 per week	—

Some points that the students might need help with:

— there are some gaps in the table (i.e. the students need to be told that they will not be able to fill in all the spaces)
— the meaning of the term 'social activities' (arguably this could include sports activities)
— the descriptions of language-learning facilities (e.g. 'self-access study centres'). However, it is best to let them try to work out what these are before offering help.
— the difference between words with related meanings (e.g. 'canteen' and 'dining room')

Task 2

Students who decide to describe their own kind of school could be asked to complete a table like the one in Task 2.

Another task would be to ask students to write a letter in pairs to the school of their choice requesting any further information they felt they needed.